# Cycling
# in
# The Cotswolds

Stephen Hill

**Published by Sigma Leisure** – an imprint of
Sigma Press, 1 South Oak Lane, Wilmslow, Cheshire SK9 6AR, England.

**British Library Cataloguing in Publication Data**
A CIP record for this book is available from the British Library.

**ISBN:** 1-85058-354-4

**Typesetting and Design by:** Sigma Press, Wilmslow, Cheshire.

**Maps by:** Stephen Hill

**Illustrations:** Clive Parsons

**Cover by:** Orbit Design

**Printed and Bound by**
Manchester Free Press, Unit E3, Longford Trading Estate, Thomas Street,
Stretford, Manchester M32 0JT. Telephone 061 864 4540

# PREFACE

In 1985 when I established a cycle hire and holiday business covering the area featured in this guide, I soon discovered the need for information on good cycling routes in the Cotswolds. After several years of ragged maps, highlight pens, and hand-written iteneraries, and many apologies to visitors for the region's lack of published welcome for cyclists, something had to be done.

While there are now published routes, some of which I have had a hand in, they are for rides within each county. This book covers the region without reference to such boundaries and will, I hope, enable visitors on bicycles to enjoy the whole of this renowned tourist area.

Cyclists have special requirements. Firstly, the cyclist needs to be assured of as safe a ride as possible; 'A' roads are crossed rather than followed, right turns minimised and entry to the larger towns is by the most cycle-friendly route.

Secondly, the choice of village, castle, church or other attraction needs to be dictated by the ease of access by cycle. There is little hope of a pleasant ride if a destination is selected without reference to the major roads or motorways that may surround it.

Thirdly, the route should follow itself. By this I mean that your way should flow, and follow the terrain rather than fight it. This gives a coherent and satisfying ride.

Using these guidelines I have chosen a selection of my favourite rides. Included are both personal points of view and descriptions of features and historical references that have struck me as unusual, interesting or representative, and some of more well-known treasures of the region.

A guide to an area so wealthy in attractions and quiet lanes inevitably leaves out as much as it includes. Once you have followed some of my recommendations I hope that you will feel confident in constructing your own rides.

Many thanks to Clive Parsons for the pen and ink drawings. I was lucky to have asked for them in the winter; the summer would have seen him cycling every free daylight hour! Thanks also to the wrecked bike I rescued from a Cricklewood garden shed all those years ago, which, in 'doing it up' for someone, got me hooked on cycling.

*Stephen Hill.*

# CONTENTS

## *BACKGROUND*

**Coverage and Location Maps** ix, x

**Using this guide** 1

**A Brief introduction to the Cotswolds** 5

**Cycling through a Living Land** 7

**The Bicycle as Transport** 11

**Cycling by Train** 15

**Notes especially, but not exclusively, for overseas visitors** 16

## *ROUTES*

**1. Snowshill or 'Snozzle'?** 21

*Broadway, Snowshill, Broadway Tower, Willersley, Broadway.*
*11 miles*

**2. '. . . The Bells They Sound So Clear. . .'** 28

*Broadway, Childswickham, Hinton Cross, Elmley Castle, Little Comberton, Great Comberton, Bredon's Norton, Westmancote, Kemerton, Overbury, Conderton, Beckford, Dumbleton, Wormington, Aston Somerville, Childswickham, Broadway.*
*28 miles*

**3. 'The Wife that survived, the Abbey that didn't' 36**

*Winchcombe, Sudeley, Hailes, (Didbrook, Stanway, Didbrook), Winchcombe*
*10 miles.*

**4. 'Wool, Falcons and Fish' 43**

*Moreton-in-Marsh, Lower Lemington, Dorn, Draycott, Broad Campden, Chipping Campden, Broad Campden, Blockley, Batsford, Moreton-in-Marsh.*
*15 miles*

**5. 'Edgehill and a Windmill' 50**

*Moreton-in-Marsh, Todenham, Willington, (Shipston-on-Stour), Upper Tysoe, Edgehill, Kineton, Moreton Paddox, Wellesbourne, (Stratford-upon-Avon), Walton, Pillerton Priors, Fullready, Halford, Armscote, Illmington, Ebrington, Paxford, Aston Magna, Batsford, Moreton-in-Marsh.*
*43 miles*

**6. 'Gloucestershire into Oxfordshire: the Valley around Kingham' 58**

*Moreton-in-Marsh, Evenlode, Broadwell, Upper Oddington, Bledington, Idbury, Fifield, Milton-under-Wychwood, Lyneham, Kingham, Dalesford, Adlestrop, Evenlode, Moreton-in-Marsh.*
*26 miles*

**7. 'Towards the Thames: the Lower Windrush' 66**

*Burford, Widford, Asthall, Minster Lovell, Crawley, (Whitney), New Yatt, North Leigh, Fawler, Finstock, Mount Skippett, Leafield, Asthall Leigh, Swinbrook, Fulbrook, Burford.*
*23 miles*

**8. 'Old Hooky and the Whispering Knights' 73**

*Charlbury, Spelsbury, Enstone, Little Tew,(Great Tew), Ledwell, Nether Worton, Barford St.Michael, South Newington, Wigginton, Sidford Ferris, Hook Norton, Churchend, Little Rollright, Over Norton, Chipping Norton, Chadlington, Charlbury.*
*37 miles*

**9. 'Bosworth Flag and Tenpenny Nails to Eat' 81**

*Oxford, Cumnor, Appleton, Longworth, Hinton Waldrist, (Duxford, Chimney, Aston), Pusey, Buckland, Tadpole Bridge, Bampton, Aston, Yelford, Hardwicke, Stanton Harcourt, Swinford, Cumnor, Oxford.*

*34 miles*

**10. 'Classic Cotswolds: the Upper Windrush valley' 88**

*Bourton, Clapton-on-the-Hill, Sherborne, Windrush, Little Barrington, Burford, Taynton, Great Barrington, Great Rissington, Little Rissington, Bourton-on-the-Water.*

*21 miles*

**11. 'A coupla Swells and Slaughters' 95**

*Bourton-on-the-Water, Lower Slaughter, Upper Slaughter, Lower Swell, Upper Swell, Donnington brewery, Condicote, Ryknild Street, Upper Slaughter, Bourton-on-the-Water.*

*14miles*

**12. 'A Sheep in a Church, and a Crocodile' 101**

*Bourton-on-the-Water, Farmington, Northleach, Coln St.Dennis, Fossebridge, Chedworth villa, Cassey Compton, Compton Abdale, Hazleton, Turkdean, Notgrove, Cold Aston, Bourton-on-the-Water.*

*25 miles*

**13. 'A Little Bit of Hell of the North Cotswolds' 109**

*(Bourton-on-the-Water) Upper Slaughter, Condicote Lane, Condicote, B4077, (Taddington), B4077, Sudeley Hill, Roel Gate, Syreford, Shipton, Salperton, Notgrove, Turkdean, Cold Aston, Notgrove, Harford, Upper Slaughter, (Bourton-on-the-Water).*

*31 miles*

**14. 'The White Way' 115**

*Cirencester, North Cerney, Woodmancote, (Colesbourne), Winston, Duntisbourne Abbots, Duntisbourne Lear, Middle Duntisbourne, Duntisbourne Rous, Daglingworth, Baunton, Cirencester.*

*20 miles*

**15. 'Akeman Street'** **122**

*Akeman Street: Cirencester, Siddington, South Cerney, Cerney Wick, Down Ampney, Kempsford, Whelford, (Fairford), Southrop, Eastleach Turville, Eastville Martin, Holwell, Coln St.Aldwyns, Quenington, Ready Token, Siddington, Upper Siddington, Cirencester.*

*38 miles*

**16. 'Railways, Canals and a Man-Eating Monster'** **129**

*Malmesbury, Milbourne, Garsden, Somerford Common, Minety, Lower Moor, Upper Minety, Oaksey, Kemble, Ewen, Coates, Tarlton, Rodmarton, Culkerton, Ashley, Long Newnton, BrokenBorough, Malmesbury.*

*31 miles*

**17. 'Two hidden valleys and a Glimpse of the Sea'** **138**

*Malmesbury, Foxley, Easton Grey, Westonbirt, Newington Bagpath, Kingscote, (Owlpen, Uley) Wotton-under-Edge, Wortley, Alderley, Hillerlesey, Hawksbury, Horton, Little Sodbury, Old Sodbury, Coombes End, Doddington, Doddington Ash, Tormarton, Acton Turville, Little Drew, Grittleton, Hullavington, Norton, Foxley, Malmesbury.*

*48 miles*

**18. 'Strutting Stroud'** **149**

*Stroud, cycle path, Nailsworth, Nympsfield,(Hetty Pegler's Tump), Coaley, Frocester, Leonard Stanley, Stonehouse, cycle path, Stroud.*

*17 miles*

**19. 'Tower to Tower to Tower'** **156**

*Oxford to Bath, via Bourton-on-the Water, Ilmington and Cherington*

*156 miles (in four sections)*

**Appendix** **174**

*List of Tourist Information Centres in the Cotswolds, and advice on getting the most from them.*

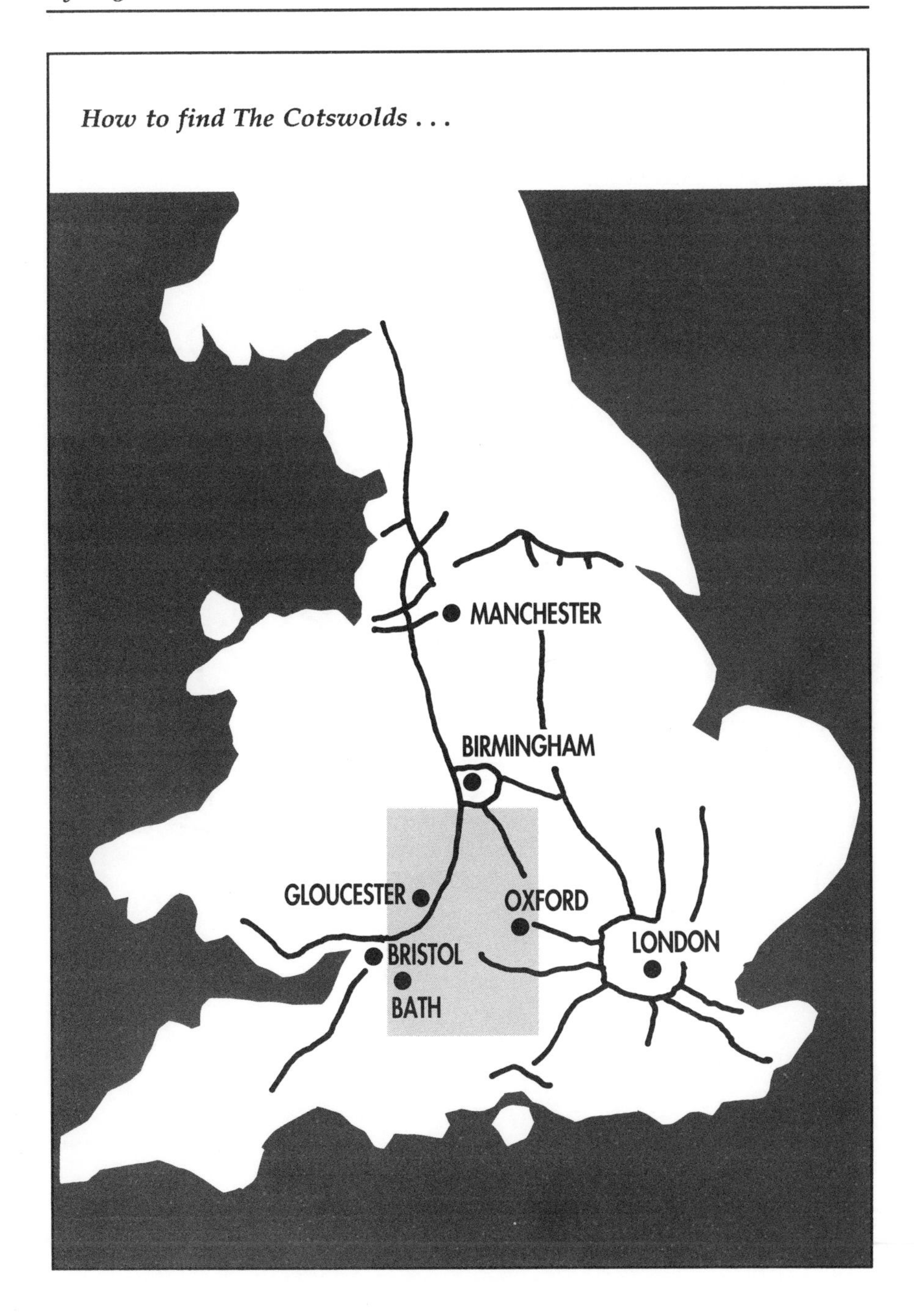
How to find The Cotswolds . . .
MANCHESTER
BIRMINGHAM
GLOUCESTER
OXFORD
LONDON
BRISTOL
BATH

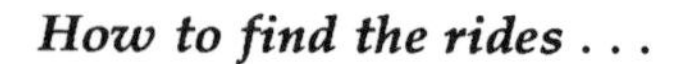
How to find the rides . . .

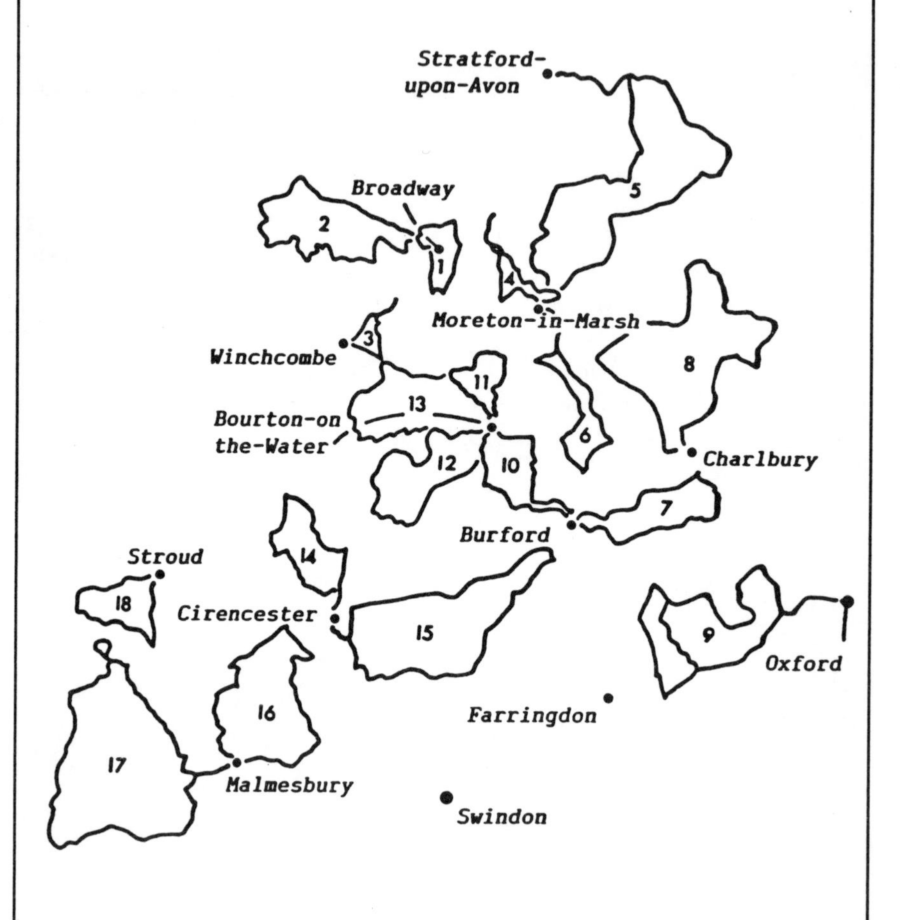
Stratford-
upon-Avon
Broadway
Moreton-in-Marsh
Winchcombe
Bourton-on
the-Water
Charlbury
Burford
Stroud
Cirencester
Oxford
Farringdon
Malmesbury
Swindon
Bath
1
2
3
4
5
6
7
8
9
10
11
12
13
14
15
16
17
18

# USING THIS GUIDE

This section is designed to help you get the best use from the information contained in each route.

## Format

All the routes, except the Oxford to Bath trip, are circular. This means that they return you to your start point! Some you will easily manage in a day, while others are either longer, or have so much to see, that you would do well to take a couple of days to complete them.

Most routes run anti-clockwise. This cuts down on the need for right-hand turns, which, in this country, are more dangerous than left-hand ones.

Each ride begins with the following categories which should give you a feel for the route:

✓ Brief Description

✓ Distance

✓ Terrain

✓ Rail Access

✓ Links With . . .

✓ Cutting It Short

✓ Route

This information, together with the coverage map, will help you find the ride, or rides, that are suitable for your fitness, how much time you want to spend at the attractions on the way, the total time you have to spend on the trip and the area you most wish to explore. If you cross reference the routes, together with the coverage map, you'll be able to link neighbouring rides together.

Each ride gives a narrative description of the route and a basic map. You may find that this is all you need to find your way with ease. A more detailed can be of help, and will also provide additional information of neighbouring roads and features of the landscape that will aid route-finding.

Please note that total distances are accurate; if in doubt, they have been rounded up to the nearest whole mile. Instructions in the narrative: "turn left in 400 yards", "continue for half a mile" are for guidance only. These distances have been estimated, or may indicate how far it 'feels' from one point to another.

Besides highlighting points of interest along the way, every route also features more detailed descriptions of selected castles, museums and historical references. Using the bibliography to find more specialist books on various aspects of history, countryside or geology will glean further fascinating details of the country you cycle through.

Finally, you may find it useful to photocopy the details of the route you wish to follow and carry that with you on the road; if it gets wet (though it never rains on cyclists in the Cotswolds!) you haven't ruined your book, and a loose leaf is easier to handle while cycling than a bound book. A separate sheet will also fit neatly into a bar bag top or other plastic wallet.

## Churches

You will find hundreds of churches mentioned in the guide, both in the more detailed descriptions, and in the route narrative; I make no apology for this.

I am not personally religious and seldom visit a church to attend a service. But for a living illumination of the history, culture and life of a community there is nothing better than to find the church. They have been used not only for worship but also as hiding places, sources of official sanctuary, temporary prisons and even as emergency grain stores. For centuries the parish was also the administrative unit of local government. Churches are the buildings least likely to be demolished or severely altered, even if their use is changed. "Left by the shop" or "right by the post office" are not as enduring directions as those featuring a church.

When many earlier churches were first built they were often the only solid stone construction in the village. Houses were built by the rest of the community to cluster around the spiritual heart of the settlement.

Sometimes you will see churches alone by the side of a lane or even in the isolated middle of a field. This often means that the rest of the village has now disappeared, or moved to be near a more recent church. In other cases the church is by, or even attached to a manor or other grand house. Sometimes this is to provide a family chapel. But it can also show an attempt at a rather unpleasant 'ownership' of piety by the wealthy original builders. If giving money to the church increased the possibility of salvation, what might be gained by giving a whole church?

Churches are particularly useful to the cyclist as a waymark or signpost. The Saxon, Norman, or later builders often chose prominent sites; on a ridge, a hilltop or overlooking a stream. Sometimes the spire or tower can be seen miles away and you can do without the need for a map entirely. Churches were designed to be imposing both as structures and as a symbol of the power of the 'Word' and its authority over the people of the area.

Though a church may date back for over 1000 years, and may be on an even older site, most are still a living and changing centre for the community. Not as many people may attend each Sunday, but 'hatches, matches and dispatches', births, marriages and deaths, usually involve the church even among non-attenders. They are not stagnant places and many will have, say, a newly sewn altar cloth or a mural made by the local school.

## Access

Many churches will be open for you to enter as you wish. Some will be locked but will have clear details of where to find the key-holder. Others will be sadly locked and have no clue as to where to find the key. In this case you can always try the nearest house. Another category is the redundant church. This is a formal title which shows that the church authorities are officially no longer able to justify holding services there. If the building has historical or archaeological value, these are sometimes adopted by the Redundant Churches Fund who will always give access details.

Once you have looked around do remember to close the door and return the key if you borrowed one. Don't forget to pay for any guidebooks or postcards you wish to take.

Enjoy the churches of the Cotswolds. Whether you use them as art galleries, local history collections, places of reverence or only as waymarkers they will add enormously to your cycling in the area.

# A Brief Introduction to the Cotswolds

## Pre-History and History up to the Roman Invasions

The geology and geography of the Cotswolds are of course closely linked. You will not find the great Lake Harrison on any map, since it appeared during the Ice Ages. It covered the Vale of Evesham all the way over to the Malvern hills to the west and way up what is now the Stour valley, to the north, where it was hemmed in by a wall of ice. It was fed by the waters of the Thames and Severn which were then far wider and deeper. It is peculiar to think of sitting at the top of Broadway Hill with the waters of the great lake lapping at your feet.

Lake Harrison was eventually frozen for many centuries and a vast sheet of ice covered the north-western area as far as Moreton-in-Marsh. It then melted again and the effect of the waves can still be seen in the stepped ridge on the side of the escarpment from Moreton-in-Marsh to Fenny Compton. When the ice became water again for the last time, around 10,000 years ago, Lake Harrison simply drained away.

The physical make up of the Cotswolds was then quite similar to the way it is now. The flora and fauna have however evolved, affecting the appearance of the area. Coverings of trees can prevent erosion; more open areas can more easily be grazed leading to closer and shorter vegetation which does not allow the soil to be held in place so well.

For around 5,000 years man had little effect. About 4,000 B.C. the climate altered, becoming drier and warmer, allowing the 'immigrants' from Europe to become more settled herdsmen and farmers rather than hunter-gatherers.

The barrows (burial chambers) that these people built are the oldest monuments to their culture. One has been dated to 2800 B.C. Hetty Pegler's Tump and Belas Knap, both of which are on, or close to, routes in this guide, are excellent examples of these barrows. They not only contained human bones but also those from deer, wolves, wild cats and other animals. Remains of horses have also been found, which shows that there were some areas of the higher Cotswolds that were always clear of trees, providing the open country suitable for these animals.

The discovery of smelting which brought in the Bronze Age just before 2000 B.C. lead to more sophisticated constructions, appropriate for a more highly developed culture. The Rollright Stones, with the King Stone aligned with the sun, came from this period. Whether the many traditions, strange tales and fertility rites associated with such structures are survivals from this period, handed down through the generations, is doubtful, but they do show that we remain fascinated by the spiritual and unknown.

In the middle of the Bronze Age, c.1600 B.C., the climate changed for the worse ('climate change' is nothing new; man's effect on it is), and the people who then lived in the Cotswolds reacted by becoming more settled. Aerial pictures can highlight the faint lines of field boundaries from this period, over 3000 years ago. Though usually more recent, in many fields that you will cycle by, at certain times of the year and with the right light, you will notice a change of the colour of a crop, or a raised line, suggesting the position of a boundary ditch. Even some of the bridleways in the area, the 'hollow-ways', with trees on either side forming a clear path protected from the worst of the weather, especially the snow, are likely to date from this time.

When the peoples of the south of England became better at organising themselves for survival, and showed signs of established communities, they had time for to develop less attractive human characteristics. The travel of individuals or small groups for trade became the movement of whole tribes to attack, seize and conquer their neighbours. The first large scale arrivals came from northern Europe bringing new technologies, and the ability to work with iron in particular. The area around the Cotswolds had everything needed for iron smelting, so the area became much fought over. The invaders had used iron to make their weapons and thus were better equipped than their local opponents.

The next series of attacks probably came from the tribes of Cornwall who moved steadily eastwards, taking existing camps as they went. It is these people who occupied Bredon Hill, featured on another of our rides. The warriors from the west didn't have it all their way however and other fortifications were built by the locals. The ramparts in the remains of the Wychwood, passed on two other rides, come from this fight back.

Further threats to our original Cotswold inhabitants came from the east, where the Belgic tribes had learnt new ways of fighting from their struggles against the Romans in their native Germany and Belgium. So the first contact that the south of England had with the Romans was not Caesar saying 'Veni, vidi, vici' but once removed through previous opponents of the Roman legions moving northward. These were the Dobunni who made their local base at what is now Cirencester.

When the Romans themselves arrived in the area they built roads, one of the first being Akeman Street, the heart of another route in this guide.

You will pick up much greater detail on the Roman occupation from the recommended museums and villas that you cycle past. One point is important to make, however.

It is easy to think of the Romans simply marching in, killing, burning and destroying. They were far more clever than this. One reason for their success was that they imposed their rule through trade and assimilation. It is simply not efficient to leave hundreds of broken and angry communities at your back. The local traders and farmers of the Cotswolds were soon supplying the Romans with their food and materials, and from a business point of view probably had far more regular and larger orders than in the 'good old days' before the Romans came.

The movement of peoples did not halt once the Romans had established themselves. But since the story of the subsequent changes is told in surviving objects, churches, artefacts and communities, further detail here is unnecessary. Take time to stop on your ride to explore what you pass, and the more recent history of the Cotswolds will come alive for you.

What is worth examining here is the life of real, average local men and women whose lives are often ignored by the history books.

## Cycling through a Living Land: the more recent history of The Cotswolds

Cycling around this area today, you will have the sense of a generally prosperous region. Commerce is now based on a combination of tourism, agriculture, a little light industry, with each town serving the needs of the local community around by providing shops, doctor, libraries and so on. Many communities have also become dormitory towns for larger neighbouring towns or cities, or even worse, weekend retreats for second home owners. A local man in Lower Swell recently hoped that the trains to Moreton-in-Marsh would speed up; this would allow 'real' commuters to move in, taking over from the second home owners who hardly lived in his village at all. This is a very modern distinction. In towns such as Broadway the local people are often moved to the estates on the outskirts of the settlement, leaving the honey coloured cottages to 'incomers'. This is often preferred; the prettiest cottages can be difficult and expensive to live in and maintain.

Finally it is important to realise that the Cotswolds are still changing, as they always have done. Only in the last few years for example, has oil-seed rape been added to the range of crops in the area. Its bright yellow flower and asthma provoking pollen are now a common sight, partly due to the E.E.C. and the common agricultural policy. In the same way that changes in fashion, falling wool prices or the introduction of newly invented machinery, all external forces, have had an impact on the life of the Cotswolds and its prosperity, the 1990s are adding to the story of the Cotswolds.

## The Picture Postcard Image of The Cotswolds

If you say 'the Cotswolds' the image that is created, even for people from the other side of the world, is of a village with a stream, including the cottages, an ancient and well-kept church, and carefully selected garden flowers against the perfect background of the local, honey-coloured stone.

But wait a minute. This image is recent, and has only been sustainable for less than fifty years.

William Cobbett, who wrote his 'Rural Rides' in 1826, said of the area: "This wold is in itself an ugly country . . . having less to please the eye than any other I have seen. The sub-soil here is a yellowish ugly stone. The houses are all built with this; and it being ugly, the stone is made white by a wash of some sort or other". Though some of this vehemence can be put down to Cobbett having one of his frequent bad days, he was not alone in his view.

Another writer of the same period, Rev. John Skinner from Somerset, wrote that "The views on each side presented nothing deserving of record" of his journey from Cirencester to Birdlip. While an earlier comment from Ralph Bigland, writing in 1791 "The Prospect is much too regular to be very picturesque" shows an even longer term dissatisfaction with the area.

For the people who lived and worked in the area life was tough. It was very far from the image of rosy-cheeked farm workers gathered happily around the village green or chatting outside the public house. The villages on top of the hills were made cold by the wind ("Stow-on-the-Wold where the wind blows cold" as the rhyme says), while those in the valleys were damp as well. The very conditions that were ideal for working wool and silk were uncomfortable for living in.

Fuel for keeping warm or for cooking with was also difficult to find. The bareness of the wolds, which was essential for grazing sheep, provided few trees for firewood. The nearest coal mines, in Kent or the Forest of Dean, were too far away to provide economic or regular supplies, at least before the arrival of the railways. (The coal merchants that now appear almost accidentally sited by some railway stations, originally depended on the train for their supplies.) If keeping warm was a problem, power for milling corn, or processing wool was easier to obtain from wind or water mills. This was however for profit, not for the benefit of the people, or the quality of their lives. As late as the 1930's just 17% of Cotswold houses had electricity, and only 4% had a bathroom.

The average diet was poor, the better of the provisions being taken by the land owners, or sold to travellers at the coaching inns on the main thorough-fares. Ghoulish selections of man traps can be seen in many of the area's museums; the land-owners would go to any length to protect 'their' game or rabbits. Some inhabitants were more fortunate, and had the right to an occasional deer or brace of pheasants, but this was always in the gift of the estate owners or managers.

So the view the Cotswolds present today has been created by what could be called the five invasions. These would be the ice and water that created much of the landscape you see, the Romans who changed the environment more than any other group for a thousand years, the sheep, for whose benefit the flora and fauna was altered, the railways and canals, which enabled the transport of people and goods in a far greater quantity than before, and finally the tourists for whom the landscape, and services have been further changed.

# 'A Footnote in History'

One invasion and revolution that was forecast, but sadly failed to happen was that of the bicycle:

> *"It is probable that the bicycle will cause a larger demand for remote country houses. To the writer, who previously to this summer had never experienced the poetry of motion which the bicycle coasting downhill, with a smooth road and a favourable wind, undoubtedly constitutes, the invention seems of the greatest utility. It brings places sixty miles apart within our immediate neighbourhood.*
>
> *Let the south wind blow and we can be in quaint old Tewkesbury, thirty miles away, in less than three hours. A northerly gale will land us at the 'Blowing Stone' and the old White Horse of Berkshire with less labour than it takes to walk a mile. Yet in the old days these twenty miles were a great gulf fixed between the Gloucestershire natives and the 'chaw-bacons' over the boundary.*
>
> *Their very language is as different as possible. To this day the villagers who went to the last 'scouring of the horse' and saw the old-fashioned backsword play, talk of the expedition with as much pride as if they had made a pilgrimage to the Antipodes".*
>
> *- Joseph Gibbs, writing in 'A Cotswold Village', published in 1897.*

What a shame that his prediction that the bicycle would increase the call for country houses was spoiled by the arrival of the car.

# The Bicycle as Transport

## Travelling with a Bicycle

If you mostly use your bike for popping down to the shops, commuting or local day rides, then your first few attempts at touring with the luggage that you'll need will be an education. Detailed advice on what you do and don't need will be best found at your local cycle shop and by picking the brains of more experienced cycle tourers. A few tips based on my experience may be of use.

## What to take

First, take as little as you can. When running cycle holidays, I found the people who turned up with endless bags of luggage, and spent ages selecting what they needed to cycle with, usually came back rather shame-faced. No, they had not completed the circuit we had planned together; no, they had not needed the three-piece suit, nor the third pair of shoes.

The clients who bounced up to the workshop with only a shoulder bag, the contents of which they transferred to the panniers in minutes, were the ones who easily had time for each day's ride and explored the castle, and had time for a cream tea and still had a clean T-shirt for the journey home!

## Don't forget the three socks

A mad keen cyclist I met in Scotland several years ago was covering over 80 miles a day, staying in Youth Hostels, and carrying everything he needed in a small saddlebag. He was only able to travel this sort of distance by cutting down on the weight he carried. He was particularly proud of his socks; he had three. Not three pairs you understand, but three socks. One would be clean on, one dirty on and one would be drying in the wind on the back of his bike. I'm not suggesting that you go this far, or that you need to be uncomfortable or Spartan. 'If in doubt, leave it out' is a good maxim, however. A trial packing, followed by a few miles of cycling will soon tell you whether you have judged it well. Better to learn this beforehand, rather than halfway through your precious weekend.

## Fitting it all in

A tip on packing your panniers: when you pack a rucksack, it is good practice to put heavy items at the top. Cycle panniers require the opposite treatment. Put your heavy things at the bottom of the bags, and evenly distributed between left and right. A pair of heavier shoes for some walking can be split one shoe either side and so on. This prevents the swaying, wobbling and even breakage of the pannier rack which can result if the centre of gravity is too high.

## What to wear

One set of clothes for cycling in, one for the evening, and something for sleeping in, is a good basis for selecting clothing. A set of waterproofs, (though skin is the best waterproof in warm conditions), hat and light gloves are a wise addition at any time of the year. If you take them, you hopefully won't need them; if you don't, you will. You are not cycling in the Sahara nor the Arctic; if you need an extra T-shirt or a new pair of socks, you should be able to buy them. Add a camera if you wish, books (heavy) if you must and a couple of plastic rubbish bags (essential: very light, can be used to waterproof supposedly 'waterproof' panniers, separate dirty clothes, store wet shoes, serve as a table-cloth for a picnic, protect your B & B's carpets and so on).

# Tools

This is not a repair manual. But a reminder to take a few essentials may be useful. A spanner that fits your bicycle, a puncture repair kit (for repairing American 'flats') and a pump are the basics. A spare inner tube, again one that fits your bike, weighs little and can save time and trouble. A set of Allen keys of the right sizes would be the next addition. A long, rear, brake cable will serve as a repair for the shorter front one; as an emergency repair you can also use this to replace a broken gear cable. A small plastic bag containing a selection of the nuts, bolts and washers that hold on mudguards and racks is also a good idea. It weighs very little, and the loss of that tiny part can be as disabling as a puncture.

Beyond this collection of tools and spares your kit becomes one suitable for cycling across the far wider terrain than you'll find in the Cotswolds. If you want to take more gadgets then do so. None of the rides in this book takes you so far away from a cycle shop or other source of help. Set out with a well-maintained cycle and you'll have few problems. If your cycle is not in a good state then what are you doing anyway?

The final essential is to know how to use the tools you take. Simply carrying them around with you won't ward off punctures or other troubles.

# Cycling by Train

Many of the routes start and finish at a railway station. The combination of the train and bicycle is a marriage made in heaven; the train takes you to the overall area you wish to explore while the cycle will take you with precision to exactly the spot you want to see.

Unfortunately, British Rail under current management and government policies sees the cycle and its owner as a nuisance. At a recent meeting on transport a colleague summed it up by asking why did he and his cycle, so insignificant and ignored on the road, assume such monumental proportions as soon as they approached a train!

Some types of trains can carry several cycles, others none. The time of travel can also govern whether you will be able to cycle by train. You may have to book, and pay, in advance. Don't let any of this put you off. The combination is excellent, and it is worth reminding B.R. that a demand does exist.

Finally, if you do have problems with your cycle and the train, a smile, a 'please' and a 'thank you' can work wonders. It really is not the conductor or driver who make the rules or design the trains.

Having run a cycle business based at a station for several years I know that most B.R. staff are good people and will help if they can.

# Notes especially, but not exclusively, for Overseas Visitors

The first difference is that we drive on the 'wrong' side of the road. It is easy to know this, and get used to our strange ways, but you may revert to your training at exactly the wrong time.

I was out with a party of Americans near Bourton-on-the-Water who were doing fine; a tractor came slowly up the narrow lane confronting one of my charges. She moved to her right, and the driver to his left, to escape one another, and both ended up almost in the hedge, only feet apart, bewilderment on both faces. Take your first miles slowly and get off and walk if you feel worried at junctions or in traffic.

I realise that I've suggested that you take your first 'miles' slowly, so this seems a good point to mention miles and kilometres, in case you are used to the later.

The figures under 'Distance' are given in both miles and kilometres. In the directions only miles and yards are used. Since these are only estimates you won't go far wrong if you take yards to be metres. a quarter of a mile is about 400 metres; half a mile, 800 metres, and one mile, 1600 metres.

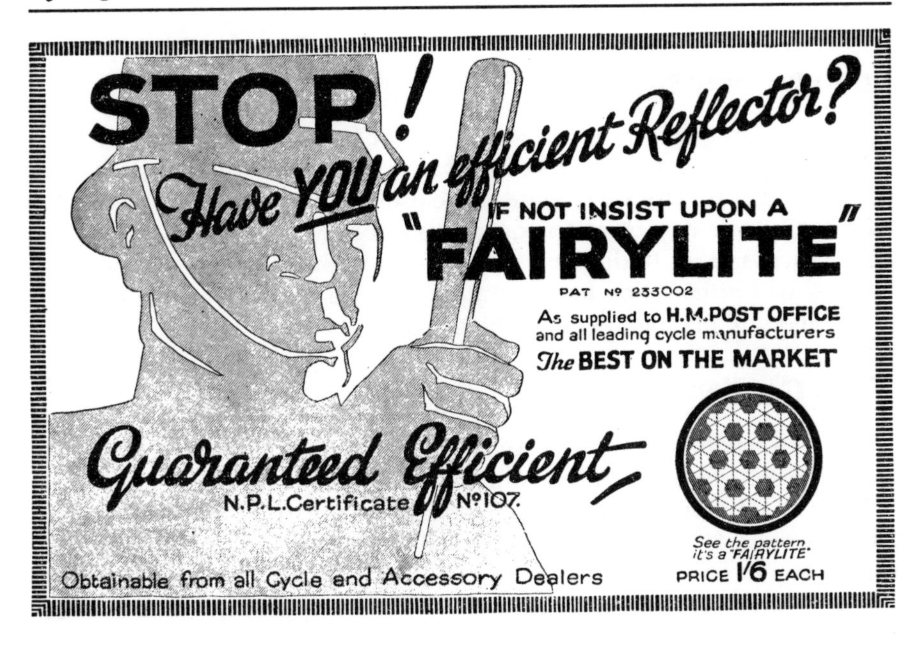


## The Law

Our Highway Code allows cyclists to ride two abreast. You should be sensible about when you use this right. The best routine in quiet lanes is to ride side-by-side but always look, and more importantly listen, for cars. When one of you hears one approaching, shout 'Oil', 'Car', 'Fumes' or whatever you wish, and break into single file to allow the vehicle to pass. You can then form a bunch again once it has gone. In towns and busy junctions you should stick to single file, no matter what your rights are. Cars are bigger and harder than you: 'Danger! Soft vehicle.'

## Security – 'Lock it or Lose it'

In towns and cities you should always lock your bike, preferably to something, rather than just to itself. You can use your discretion about locking up in the countryside and when popping into village churches and so on. It is seldom necessary to remove your pannier bags, even in towns. I would recommend that you use a bar-bag or other small piece of luggage to keep all your valuables in and take that with you WHEREVER you go. This should contain your money, travel tickets and passport.

## Opening Hours

These are a frequent cause of bewilderment for visitors from abroad. In the towns of the Cotswolds most shops are open during the day, all day, from Monday to Saturday. Some still close for lunch (even food shops!), others shut one day or afternoon a week for 'Early Closing Day'. This day varies and is traditional to each town. Small shops in outlying villages will either stick to this tradition or be 'modern', desperate for trade, and will open longer than expected.

## 'Time Gentlemen Please'

This is the traditional cry at pub. closing time. Pub opening hours have recently been changed but are still confusing. All pubs are now allowed to open all day. But they don't. Some will, some won't. And just because they are open and advertise food, this doesn't mean they will serve you something to eat. If you cycle up to the perfect pub, in the perfect setting, with a great appetite, and it is two minutes past two, you may be told quite firmly that they stopped serving at two! You may then be offered the delights of crisps or peanuts, or perhaps the sulky cheese roll in the corner.

The description above is not meant to cover all pubs but only to make you aware of possible starvation, or at least disappointment. I'd suggest that if you are passing a food stop which looks good, but is a little earlier on your route than you had planned, you stop and eat. An insurance policy of a packed lunch or fruit, or biscuits will allow you to be more courageous. Some pubs will now serve morning coffee or afternoon tea, as well as alcohol. Few will serve a glass of milk, and a request for this will immediately have you down as a North American eccentric!

## Avoiding a Wobbly Wheel

While a pint of fine English beer or cider, after a good mornings ride, is one of the delights of cycling in the Cotswolds, don't overdo it. Especially in hot weather you may be wise to stick to soft drinks and save sampling the local brew until the evening. Tap water, by the way, is safe for drinking in this country, if it comes from the mains. Some of it may not taste delicious but it will not make you ill. It is unnecessary to buy bottled water.

## Pronunciation

This isn't an English lesson. Some of our spelling truly is bizarre, and does nothing to help us say the word. This comes from us being such a mongrel country. Each group of invaders has brought its own language. Sometimes this replaced the former words, sometimes existing words were modified or added to, and in other cases the 'original' was kept.

The oldest word we use is probably 'avon' meaning a river. The River Avon therefore means the river river! Two other terms of equal age are 'brock', a country word for a badger, and whisky from the Gaelic meaning water of life. These all date from well before the Roman invasions.

A few tips on local pronunciation are included in the text. One other may be of use here as it often singles out the visitor for laughter. The ending 'cester' is contracted, so Gloucester is Gloster, Worcester Worster and so on. None of them approaches Glau-chester. But then we come to Cirencester which is . . . Ciren-cester! Some locals will swear that it is Sisiter, but this is not common. All this confusion comes from the Saxon ending of *Ceastre,* itself adapted from the Roman. The Normans then changed it again to avoid the 'r's, just as a French person today may find 'really righteous' difficult.

Otherwise you'll just have to have a 'bash' at words you are not sure how to pronounce. This may sound cheeky from someone from England where we have such a bad tradition of learning other languages, but it's the truth. Don't adopt our technique of simply shouting to be understood!

## Cycle Hire

I have not included a list of people who will rent you a bike, as the firms change, and the Tourist Information Centres, or British Tourist Authority will give you up-to-date list. You may have to be prepared to rent in a larger town or city, and then travel to your touring area. The quality of cycles will vary greatly. The type of bike you need will depend on the cycling you hope to do. When you are booking a bike be prepared to give the company your height or normal frame size. If they don't have an exact fit, chose one smaller than you normally ride. This is easier to adjust, and safer than struggling with a frame that is too big, even for short day rides.

## 'All Inclusive'

You should expect a pump, repair kit and basic tools to be included, though in a group you will only need to take one or two sets. Few companies will offer helmet hire. I think this is a good thing. A helmet has to fit perfectly and snugly to be of any use, and a hired helmet is unlikely to match your head, unless they have dozens to chose from. If you like to wear a helmet, and it is not compulsory here, bring your own. If you have a well loved and comfortable saddle and hope to cover many miles, you can consider bringing this with you too. Any cycle rental firm worth its salt will be happy for you to do a swap. Some firms will offer a choice of handlebars, men's or women's frames, toeclips fitted or not, and so on.

You should expect to pay a returnable deposit against damage. Sometimes in the busy season you will be asked to send this in advance to reserve the bike or bikes. The hire fee itself will become less per day the longer you hire the cycle. Some companies will give you several 'free' days on a two-week hire.

# 1. Snowshill or 'Snozzle'?

**Brief Description:** 'Snozzle' is how some local people will be heard pronouncing the name of the village at the heart of this ride – Snowshill. For a trip by cycle a stop at the museum at the manor at Snowshill is essential. It features a collection of ancient cycles, as well as a bizarre mixture of other items.

Once you have climbed the escarpment from Broadway, through Snowshill and a further rise to the highest point of the area you then have plenty of height in your back pocket, which you can 'spend' later, with a delicious descent into the Vale of Evesham, famous for its market gardens and the home of English asparagus. If you are cycling this route in late May or early June you should find some 'gras' on offer in local pubs or on sale by the roadside. Though close to the 'honeypot' village of Broadway you should find most of the roads quiet; most of the 'b's sticking to the 'A's, and the climb up Fish Hill!

**Distance**: 11 miles/18kms

**Terrain:** There is a climb up from Broadway to Snowshill, which continues a little past the village. There are views on the way up, so it is a good chance to practice your 'I'm not puffed at all; I've only got off to look at the view' pose. The section across the top is flat, while the descent into the Vale at Saintbury is exciting but needs some care.

**Rail Access:** Honeybourne on the Cotswold line is the nearest station, within 2.5 miles of Saintbury at the bottom of the escarpment. The route can be happily started from this point.

**Links With:** The route around Bredon Hill is also based on Broadway.

On the top of Saintbury Hill you are only 2 miles from Chipping Campden on the route from Moreton-in-the-Marsh.

## Route

We start from the green outside the small arcade which houses the Broadway Tourist Information Centre.

With your back to the T.I.C, turn left down the main street, turning left after a few yards. This turn is sometimes signed Snowshill, but not always! Cycle along this lane passing the newer church on your left, and leaving the hub-bub behind you very quickly. After half a mile you reach St.Eadburgha's church on your right-hand side. From here the gradient gradually increases, as do the views up the hill on your left and into the valley on your right; 1.25 miles after the church you will reach Snowshill village. Having looked around Snozzle, visited the Manor,

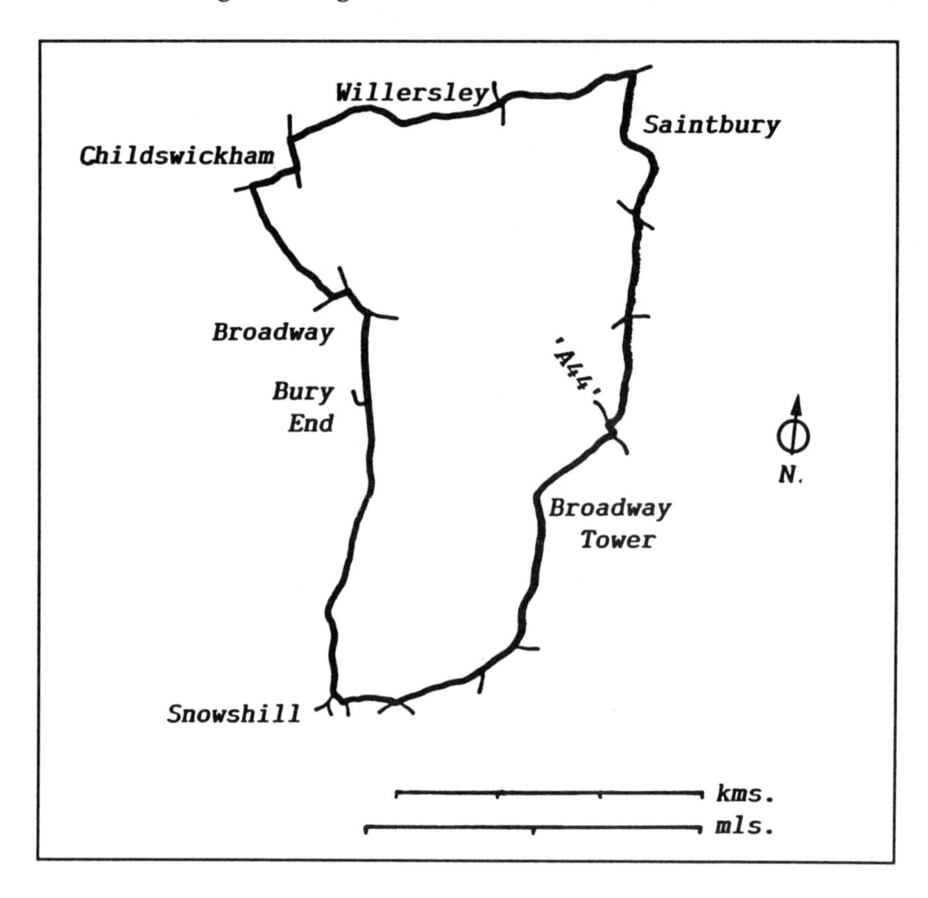

pub, or church, you leave with another small (honest!) climb. Go ahead, uphill at the first small crossroads, and then left at the second.

You are almost on top of the world at this point; the scenery, crops, air and climate all change. Go ahead at an offset junction after 400 yards, and then keep left at two more junctions. Two miles of great cycling follow, passing the Tower and park, before you reach the A44. (It is possible to turn left here as a short cut back to Broadway, but the traffic is ghastly, the views disappointing, and I'd only recommend it if a quick return is essential.) To continue, cross over the A44 with care, go ahead for half a mile and cross a small junction. At this point the hill begins to have its effect, and a lovely swoop downhill starts.

Ignore a junction halfway down (as if you could stop anyway!) and continue through Saintbury, with good buildings, to the A46. Turn left here for half a mile of 'A' road that is seldom too busy or fast. At Willersley go ahead, rather than following the 'A' road to the left. You cycle over the well preserved, but disused, railway line, and after 1 mile reach a junction with the A44. Here you turn left and then right, with CARE, after 250 yards towards Childswickham and its large church spire. Before reaching the village, however, turn left, and continue for 1 mile, again meeting the disused railway, to the A46. Turn left here and then right, with care, after 200 yards, to re-enter Broadway.

## Broadway

Broadway appears in the Doomsday Book. The village was held by the Church itself. Included in its wealth were: 'A priest and 42 villagers with 20 ploughs, 8 slaves.' A further $2^1/_2$ hides of land were the subject of a dispute: 'Urso claims back this land as the King's gift. He states he exchanged it himself with the Abbot for one manor which was of the lordship'.

Urso, a local Sheriff, must have been quite a character as he appears several times in the dry, civil servant's footnotes. You can almost hear him saying 'Now, while you're here lads, there's this couple of hides of land I want to mention . . . '

## St. Eadburgha's Church

Even if you decide not to stop and investigate this church which seems so tranquil despite being so close to the bustle of Broadway, there are features to notice as you cycle by. The good row of trees shading the churchyard from the road, the large yew bushes which are pruned away at their bases so as not to obscure the gravestones that they are threatening to engulf, and the steps by the entrance. These are unusual in that they allow you to climb over the wall to enter the churchyard, rather than use the perfectly good gate next to them. They were probably to allow people to arrive at the church by horse and dismount, or remount, with ease. Or perhaps they were built as a kind of cattle grid to make sure that wandering sheep didn't get in if the gate was accidently left open!

Inside the church there is a memorial to Sir Thomas Phillipps who saved the church from demolition, but is mainly remembered for his bibliophilic tendencies. He was a Manchester man and his money came from the cloth industry, but it all went on books and places to keep them. He printed books, filled his house with them, and even shut his wife out of the dining room to make more room for them. But when his life was running out and he realised that he would not have time to achieve his ambition he wrote 'I am buying Printed Books because I wish to have one Copy of every Book in the World!' His use of a capital 'B' in Books perhaps shows his reverence for them.

## Snowshill

**Snowshill Manor**. Henry VIII gave the manor house to Katherine Parr when he married her. It has some Tudor sections and a southern front from 1700. It is now most well known for the Magpie Museum created by Charles Paget Wade who owned the house from 1919 until his death in 1956. He renovated the house partly to provide a home for his collection. Although he doesn't name it, J.B.Priestley visited here in the Autumn of 1933 and wrote about meeting Mr.Wade in his 'English Journey'. He writes of feeling that 'life might turn into a beautiful daft fairy tale under our very noses' as he entered, and it has a similar effect today. It is like having a collection of attics on display; Samurai armour mixed with ancient musical instruments, tiny items from a dolls house next to a 'Penny Farthing' cycle. Don't expect a dry collection of carefully researched and selected objects in glass cases. Just enjoy the celebration of mans ingenuity, and one mans wish to collect examples of it.

Varied opening hours, details from: 0386 - 852410.

*The Priest's House, ground floor, Snowshill Manor*

## Broadway Tower

Built as a folly (essentially a purposeless fake) in 1793, the views really are as good as you'd imagine from such a spot. You can see parts of up to 12 counties if the visibility is good. It was in this tower that Sir Thomas Phillipps set up his printing press. William Morris and other Pre-Raphaelites used to spend their working holidays here. There are nice stories of Rossetti moaning about having to carry his food up the hill from Broadway!

Details of opening and access: 0386-852390.

## Dover's Hill

Up here on top on the world you will see to the east, your right, the ridge of Dover's Hill. This is named after Robert Dover, a lawyer by training who is remembered for establishing the Cotswold Games as an antidote to Puritanism. They were started in about 1612. "The Cotswold with the Olympic vies, In manly games and goodly exercise", as Ben Johnson wrote. The games were certainly 'manly'; shin-kicking was one of the sports. One correspondent, H.J.Massingham, tells us: "At Yabberton I heard that an old warrior used to sit and have his shins beaten by a deal plank as a form of training while one of his heroes of Campden used to 'thrape' his shins with a hammer to be deemed worthy of inclusion in the team".

Other sports included cockfighting, wrestling, horse riding and dancing. A portable wooden building was constructed, 'Dover's Castle', complete with canon to start the events and celebrate victories. The games finished in 1851 because of their rowdy reputation, and pressure from the grumpy sounding vicar at Weston-sub-Edge. They have been re-run on a couple of occasions since.

## Broadway

I don't generally recommend specific refreshment spots, but I will in the case of the Lygon Arms. Afternoon tea will set you back several pounds but I think it's worth every penny. In summer you can sit outside in the garden sipping fine tea and guzzling, sorry, nibbling delicate sandwiches and cakes. It is a stylish place and only the most outlandishly dressed cyclist will cause a raised eyebrow. Previous guests here, when it was a manor house, included both Cromwell and Charles I as their fortunes during the Civil War moved them across the country.

The hotel used to be called The White Hart, when it was one of 23 inns at the foot of the hill. Getting up Fish Hill often required a change of horses, and this made a good excuse for a break for refreshment, or even an overnight stay. General Lygon bought the inn in 1830, but it was his butler who later acquired the building, and changed its name by permission to that of his former employer.

# 2. '. . . The Bells They Sound So Clear . . .'

**Brief Description:** The title comes from A.E.Housman's poem 'In summertime on Bredon' of which more later. Although Bredon Hill is now physically separate from the Cotswold escarpment, geologically they are of the same origin. This happily allows us to include a circuit around the hill in this guide. From a distance Bredon appears a low and smooth mound, but as you'll see as you approach it has steep and rocky sides in places. Each village around the foot of the hill is distinctive; many have both churches and pubs. As you return to Broadway you also have an excellent view of the ridge of the Cotswolds from Chipping Campden to south of Winchcombe.

**Distance:** 28 miles/45 kms

**Terrain:** The ride takes you round Bredon Hill, not over it. There are some 'undulations' but nothing to tire you out. The wind can blow hard in the vale but whichever way it does the hill will protect you for some of the route. If you decide to climb to the top of the hill, then the terrain is what you'd expect!

**Rail Access:** Honeybourne is the nearest station to Broadway, just under 5 miles away. Pershore Station, also on the Cotswold line, is within 2 miles of Great Comberton and this might be the preferable place to join the ride by train.

**Links With:** The Snozzle ride is also based on Broadway. At Wormington you are within only 3 miles of Stanway on the Sudeley Castle ride.

**Cutting it Short:** Once you've committed yourself to make the circuit of the hill it's as quick to carry on as to return. Though no easier, if you do take the chance to travel up onto the top of the hill at Elmley Castle, it is possible to descend on the other side of Bredon, cycling by the only house on the very top, and then following your nose down hill. You would then regain the route at Overbury.

For a look at the hill without a full tour you could simply follow the ride to Elmley Castle and then return by the same route; the views and feel are very different even if the roads are the same.

# Route

We start outside the small arcade, Cotswold Court, which houses the Tourist Information Centre in Broadway.

With your back to the Tourist centre, turn left down the main street, continue for a busy quarter of a mile, before turning left into the A46. After 200 yards turn right, with CARE. Continue for 2 miles, through Childswickham, and leave the village by going ahead at the crossroads. Cycle on for a flat 2.5 miles to reach the A435 at Hinton Cross, which you should go straight across(!). Continue ahead for 2.5 miles to arrive at Elmley Castle. To visit the church, or for tarmac access towards the top of Bredon Hill, turn left here, up the main street. To continue, however, bear right and then left after 250 yards. In 1 mile you will reach Little Comberton, by the church; bear right here and continue for 400 yards before turning first left after leaving the village. You pass through Great Comberton in 1 mile. One mile further on there is a small turning to the right, opposite a large farm. You can see Woolas Hall up on the hill above you.

If you want to visit Nafford lock and have a fine view of the Avon, take this turn for half a mile and return. Otherwise continue at this point; cycle on for 1.25 miles to the B4080 where you turn left. This section can be fast with cars, so take care. After less than 1 mile, turn left to cycle through Bredon's Norton, then returning to the 'B' road 1 mile further on, where you turn left. In only 400 yards turn left to leave the 'B' road, and continue for 1 mile, passing through Lower Westmancote on your way, to reach Kemerton. Continue ahead through the village to pass through Overbury in half a mile. Note the stream in the pretty churchyard. Cycle on to Conderton, where you swing right with the road. Continue for a winding mile to arrive at Beckford. Visit the church and other attractions and then leave the village by turning left some 250 yards after the church. Cycle on, passing Beckford Silk, before turning right in 1 mile at a tiny crossroads. Here you cycle away from Bredon Hill, toward the lower hills of Dumbleton and Alderton.

In half a mile, having crossed a bridge over the disused railway, you reach the A435, where you turn right for a few yards, before turning left into a lane. Skirting Dumbleton Hill for 1.25 miles brings you to the village itself, where the road first swings right and then left after the

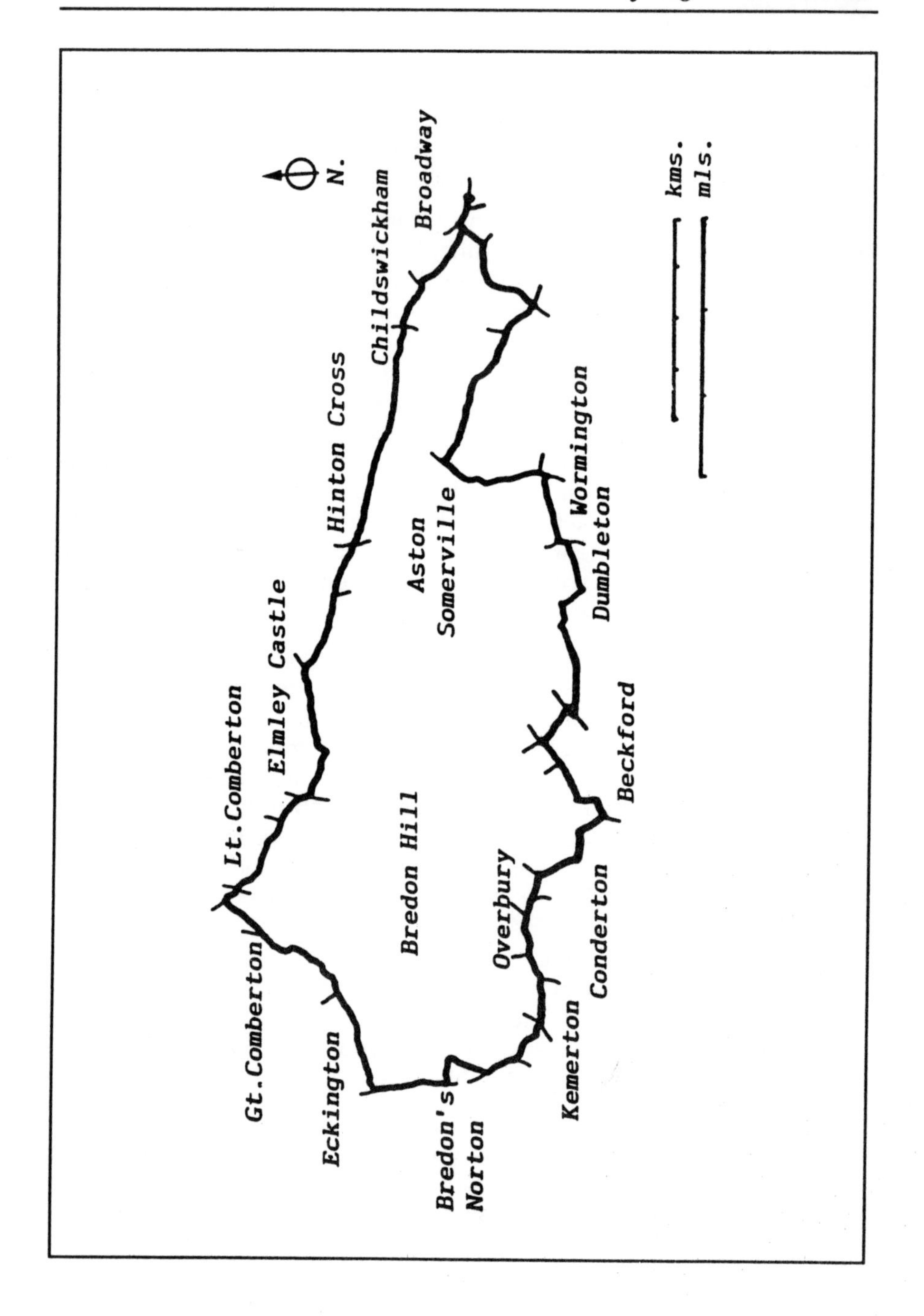
N.
Broadway
Childswickham
Hinton Cross
Aston Somerville
Wormington
Dumbleton
Elmley Castle
Lt.Comberton
Bredon Hill
Beckford
Overbury
Conderton
Gt.Comberton
Eckington
Bredon's Norton
Kemerton
kms.
mls.

church. A flat half mile brings you to the B4078 at which you turn left for 200 yards, before turning right. In under one mile you reach Wormington, and turn left at the end of the village. A quiet 1 mile's cycling brings you into Aston Somerville. Turn right through the village, passing the church to your right, and continue for 1.5 miles. At the A46, having cycled under a railway bridge, turn left. One mile of quite civilised 'A' road will see you back at Broadway, where you should turn right, with care, to regain the main street.

## Elmley Castle

There is no castle at Elmley Castle anymore. It disappeared literally piece by piece. The church contains stones taken from the castle ruins, and the old bridge at nearby Pershore was constructed with them too. There are several pubs, more than seem justified by the size of the village. One is called the Queen Elizabeth to commemorate her visit here, in August 1575, though if she spent a night at every place that she is supposed to have done she must have slept at several places each night! The font in the church at the top of the village is surrounded by writhing serpents; it's not surprising that babies often cry when they are baptised!

In the churchyard is a sundial, self supporting rather than on a wall, with several faces. It was meant to be able to give you the time anywhere in the world, or at least the Old World. According to one source, apart from during the months of October and November, it still tells the time to within eight minutes of Greenwich Mean Time. Before you ask; it's not made of quartz.

Elmley Castle provides an excellent example of the change in Cotswold villages over the last 50 years or so.

| | *houses* | *people* | *cars* |
|---|---|---|---|
| *1932* | 66 | 272 | 6 |
| *1989* | 170 | 500 | 250 |

By 1989 none of the inhabitants were farmers, and over 50 people in the village lived alone.

The small road that turns right round the Queen Elizabeth pub takes you quite a way up Bredon Hill, before the tarmac turns to a bridle-path, and is probably the best route up onto the top if the weather has been wet.

*Elmley Castle*

## 'Summertime on Bredon'

Although A.E.Housman wrote a few optimistic poems, he is best known for well crafted but rather gloomy pieces. A lovely spoof of his style and tone runs as follows:

> *"What? Still alive at twenty two,*
> *A fine upstanding man like you?*
> *If your throat's too strong to slit,*
> *Slit your girls, and swing for it".*

A further spoof starts: 'At suppertime on Bredon . . . '

You can still hear bells on Bredon, and indeed in the villages around as you cycle through. There are also exceptional views from the top. A few years ago, just after Christmas, I was up on top, and it had recently been snowing. This had cleared the air over Birmingham and whitened the peaks of the Peak District, which I could clearly see, around 80 miles away.

## Bredon

Bredon is mentioned in the Doomsday Book. Hides, hundreds, leagues and acres are all measures. The extract reads as follows:

> *"In the same Hundred the Bishop also holds Bredon. 35 hides which pay tax.*
> *In lordship 10 hides; 3 ploughs there;*
> *33 villagers and 13 smallholders with 20 ploughs. 6 slaves.*
> *A mill at 6s.8d.; meadow, 80 acres; woodland two leagues long and $1^1/_2$ leagues wide. The Bishop has it 10s. and whatever comes from it in honey and hunting and other things.*
> *Value before 1066 £10; now 10s less."*

As well as land, slaves and ploughs were obviously valuable items, and to be recorded. The Norman invaders wanted to know how much the newly conquered land was worth, and completed their survey within only 30 years of arriving. The reference to honey reminds us that it was the only source of additional sweetening, and an important constituent of mead (for the boozy old Bishop, perhaps!).

## Nafford Henge and Bredon Hill Fort

At Nafford, which you pass near by on your ride, and can also see from the top of the hill, is the site of a henge. Probably a woodhenge rather than a stonehenge, the outline is clear from aerial photographs. It was built on one of the only really flat pieces of land near the hill, in the flood plain. It was associated with the tribes encamped on the hill and was used for religious and spiritual purposes.

What has to be remembered is that several thousand years ago the land all around was wooded and wild. It was filled with dangerous and frightening animals. Some were real: wolves and bears both lived in Britain then, others such as the dragon and griffon were not, but it's easy to imagine how they were imagined to exist in such a huge, tree covered area. Their existence today in popular myths and legends shows how powerful the unknown can be. Making your home on the top of a hill, with few trees made clear sense.

Any old hill would not do. As well as considerations of visibility to keep guard from attack, and proximity of game for hunting, water is the clue as to whether a hilltop made a good home. There is still a consistent and strongly running spring near the top of Bredon, known as St.Kenelms. The Malverns, of which there are fine views from this ride, were also selected because of the water supply, this time the well is named after St.Anne. Other nearby hills without a dependable source were not used. Perhaps the naming of wells after Saints shows how importantly they were seen.

So we can see that these ancient people were similar to us. They wanted security, food, water and shelter. They also needed space for worship of some kind, which they had at Nafford.

## Beckford

Even if you ignore most of the churches on this ride do spend a moment to look at the doorway at Beckford; you don't even have to go into the church. It shows a sheaf of corn, a donkey, and a figure of Christ. It looks almost Aztec, certainly primitive, in the best sense of the word, and is as crisp as the day it was carved.

Beckford is also home to two silk businesses. One specialises in hand painting, the other in only a slightly more mechanised production of hand printing.

## Dumbleton

Dumbleton seems to me to describe perfectly the shape of this bowl-shaped hill. Perhaps it could be a new word: to dumble, or a dumbleton. This was where Sir Charles Percy, one of the supporters of the rebellion against Elizabeth I, led by the Earl of Essex, chose to retire. Many of the plotters were executed, so Sir Charles must have valued his last years in this peaceful place. Dumbleton also featured in the riots which followed 'The Golden Summer' of 1801 when a record harvest, failed to reduce prices of wheat or bread. The landowners and merchants made excessive profits instead. Haystacks were burnt and wagons attacked. The resentment of the labourers resurfaced thirty years later when the same situation occurred, this time aided by the newly introduced automatic threshing machines. The protesters were tried, and 24 men were transported to Tasmania. The folk song 'Van Diemen's Land' gives the awful details of transportation to that island. The miserable journey itself took over three months.

## Broadway

If you are returning to Broadway in the early evening it may be a calm place. The coach parties will have gone and the visitors who are staying will be eating their supper. This is a good time to see Broadway.

If you are forced to time your re-entry to the village during opening hours, and it is high season, Broadway may appear busy and cluttered. In 1937 John Moore, a well-known novelist and writer on the area, published 'The Cotswolds' and he had seen this less pleasant side of the tourist attraction:

> *"The shopkeepers smiled at me their Piccadilly smiles, so I was reminded of the old nursery rhyme:*
>
> *Will you come into my parlour?*
> *Said the Spider to the Fly*
>
> *I smiled too, and walked on. I had been to Broadway before. I thought that I should like to write out a notice in big letters and carry it through Broadway on a sandwich-board, a notice like this:*
>
> *I AM NOT INTERESTED IN SHAM ANTIQUES. I DO NOT REQUIRE ANY OF THOSE OLD OAK CHESTS WHICH YOU MAKE SO INGENIOUSLY. I ABOMINATE ALL MANIFESTATIONS OF ARTS-AND-CRAFTS. I AM NOT A FOLK DANCER NOR A MORRIS DANCER NOR A PLAYER UPON ANY KIND OF OBSOLETE MUSICAL INSTRUMENT. PLEASE DO NOT TRY TO SELL ME ANY HAND-WOVEN SCARVES. AND I DON'T WANT ANYTHING MADE OF RAFFIA EITHER. NOR DO I WISH TO SIT ON A CHAIR WHICH WAS SAT ON BY QUEEN ELIZABETH OR TO SLEEP IN A BED WHICH WAS SLEPT IN BY KING CHARLES. ALL I WANT IS A PUB WITH A BAR WHERE I CAN BUY HALF-A-PINT OF DECENT BEER FOR FOUR-PENCE AND TALK WITH HONEST MEN. IF THERE BE ANY IN BROADWAY . . . "*

Phew! After that I would have thought that Moore would have been lucky to be served in any pub in the village.

# 3. 'The Wife that Survived, the Abbey that didn't'

**Brief Description:** Based on Winchcombe at the foot of the escarpment, this is a short ride, but with one taxing climb. Cycling into Sudeley Castle is a perfect way of arriving at this human sized home. The climb up Sudeley Hill brings special views and deep breaths, but leads via a lost lane to an exciting descent to Hailes. Though the village is known for its ruined Cistercian Abbey, the church is a real gem with intact wall paintings from the 1400s and many other attractions. A link is included through tiny Didbrook to Stanway and its impressive Manor House. The final return stretch is unavoidably along an 'A' road, though visibility is good and you are rewarded with views to the west of Dumbleton and Bredon Hills, while cycling along, tucked into the base of the Cotswold ridge.

**Distance**: 10 miles/16 kms – Taking the short cut to avoid Stanway reduces this to 6 miles/10 kms

**Terrain**: The climb up Sudeley Hill will slow you down or even allow you to walk. The surface on the lane down to Hailes can make the descent tricky. Otherwise, there are only modest gradients to reach Didbrook and Stanway. The return is level.

**Rail Access**: Apart from the restored line between Toddington and Greet, the nearest stations are either Cheltenham, or Honeybourne on the Cotswold line.

**Links With**: At the top of Sudeley Hill you are by part of the partly off-road route from Bourton-on-the-Water. Stanway is 3 miles away from Wormington on the round Bredon Hill ride.

**Cutting It Short**: This is a short ride in itself, but you can miss out the spur to Didbrook and Stanway, by simply returning to Winchcombe via the A46, just after leaving Hailes.

## Route

We start this ride from the Tourist Information point in the main street in Winchcombe.

If you want to consider using the train to help your return, why not check the timetable now? Do note that the T.I.C. here has only seasonal opening; out of season you can contact Cheltenham Tourist office.

With your back to the Tourist Office you can either go straight across the main road into the lane opposite, or cycle right for a few hundred yards and then left into a more private entrance. Assuming you take the first choice, you cycle along for a quarter of a mile, before turning towards the grounds of Sudeley Castle, through Vineyard Street, by the Cotswold stone public toilets! Continue to find the entrance to the Castle. It is permissible to cycle into the exit only lane. Having explored the castle leave by the higher exit, up the hill.

This hill soon begins to bite, although it is short, and you may wish to walk a little. Turn left by a wood after half a mile and then left again after less than half a mile, signed 'Little Farmcote'. This track can be rough in places but is secluded and away from most cars. On some maps in it known as Salter's Way, perhaps being part of the track to Droitwich, where the local salt was found. It descends rapidly after half a mile, and in another half a mile you bear right to reach Hailes. The abbey and church are a few yards to your right, up the hill. Having explored, cycle downhill again, crossing over the restored railway, to reach the A46 after half a mile. Turn right and immediately right again, with CARE. (You may prefer to walk the few yards, staying on the Hailes side of the road).

After 300 yards cycle under the railway, and a quarter of a mile later, you enter Didbrook. Leave, passing the church on your left, and half a mile later, after a dogleg, you'll have Stanway waiting down the lane ahead of you. Once you have looked around the village of Stanway, you return by retracing your outward route, through Didbrook, and as far as the turn onto the A46, which you now join to return to Winchcombe after 2 miles. An alternative to this section of 'A' road, which is seldom too busy or fast, is to take the train. This runs on the line you have cycled over and under. Because it is a tourist railway, services are not very regular, but it will take you from Toddington, half a mile from Stanway, to Greet, just north of Winchcombe.

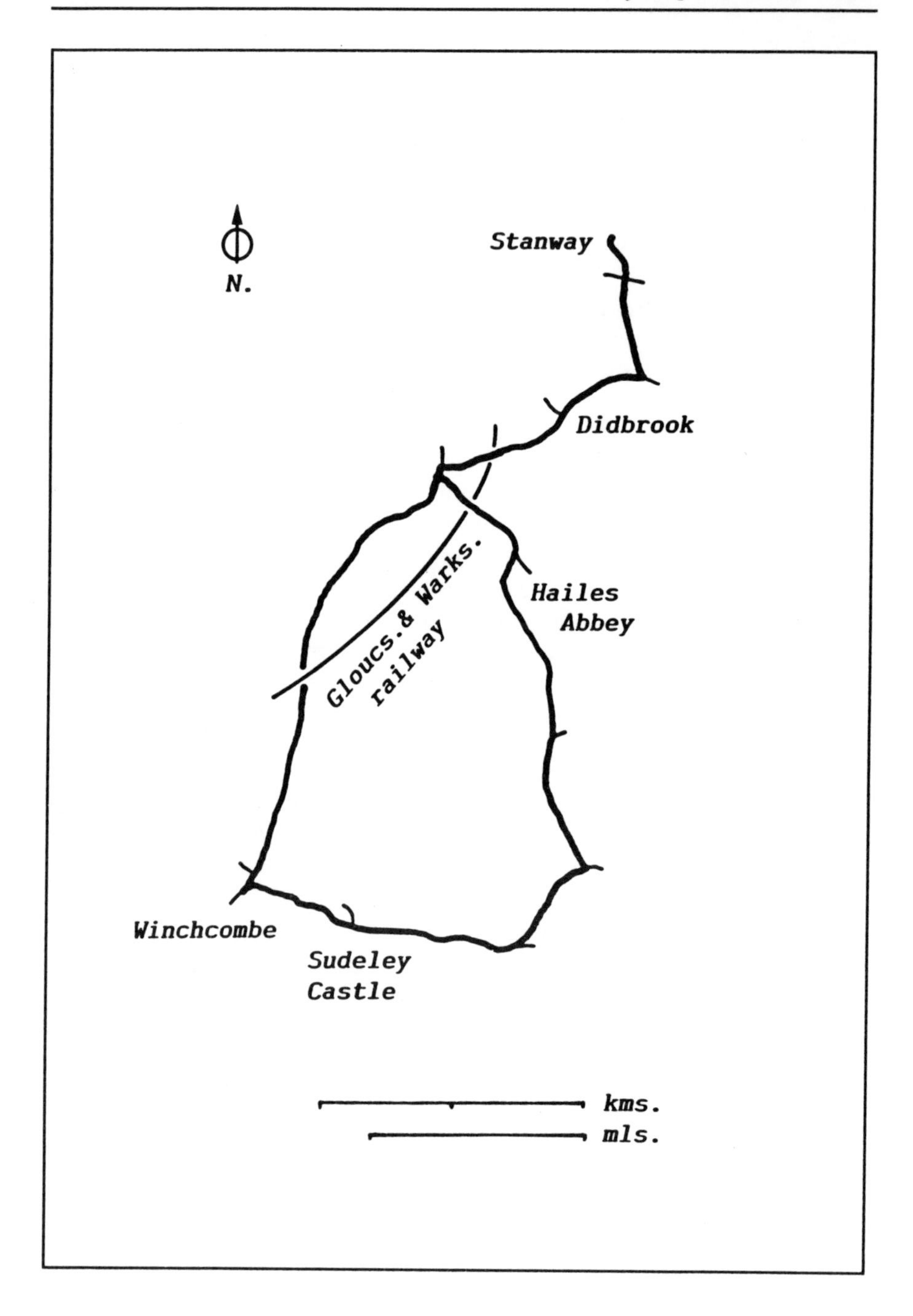
N.
Stanway
Didbrook
Gloucs.& Warks.
railway
Hailes
Abbey
Winchcombe
Sudeley
Castle
kms.
mls.

## Winchcombe

We know a lot about the history of Winchcombe. Ceonwulf lived here when he founded Hailes Abbey in 798. It was capital of Winchcombeshire until it became part of Gloucestershire in 1017. Its importance did not survive, and there are no remains of the abbey or the Royal palace. The George Inn still has 'RK' carved over its wooden entrance, standing for Richard Kidderminster who was abbot of Winchcombe from 1488 to 1525, and built The George to accommodate visitors and traders.

When you return to Winchcombe, or before you leave, look upwards to see a Winchcombe speciality. These are the mansard roofs. Rather than having only one slope to each side these have two, the lower is larger and more steeply pitched than the upper. Though not unique to Winchcombe they are clearly very popular in the town. Elsewhere, guess where, they are known as 'Cornish' roofs.

## Sudeley Castle

While some castles are so large and austere that it is difficult to imagine life in them, Sudeley Castle was, and is, designed for living in. It has not been used constantly since it was built in the 1400s; Parliamentary troops 'slighted' it (that is, made it uninhabitable) during the Civil War, and it was not lived in again until 1837. It is famous for being the home of Katherine Parr, the one wife of Henry VIII who outlived him. There are many fine pieces on show inside, but I like the more modern caricatures of writers and politicians. Do ask an attendant to explain the symbolism in the large painting by the gallery. The collection of items with royal connections was brought together by Emma Dent, whose family refurbished the castle and church. There is a rose collection, a cafe and sometimes falconry displays. Every year there is also a programme of special events ranging from recreations of Civil War encampments to musical recitals. Why not ring to find out what's on when you hope to cycle through?

The grounds open from 11am and the apartments from 12 noon, from April to October. Details from: 0242 602308.

## Hailes Abbey and Church

The Abbey was founded in 1246 by Richard, Earl of Cornwall, as a pious tribute for having survived a shipwreck. Edmund, his son, brought back a relic of Holy blood, guaranteed as genuine by Pope Urban IV. This made the name of the abbey ensuring a constant stream of pilgrims, bringing money with them.

When Henry VIII broke from Rome, he didn't care a **** what the Pope said and the relic was declared to be a fake. The abbey was largely destroyed, stones from it were used in neighbouring buildings, including Sudeley Castle. A point up on the hillside is called Cromwell's seat and is meant to be from where Thomas Cromwell watched the destruction of the abbey. The museum in the grounds has a good collection of finds from excavations of the area. They include a roof boss with a carving of Christ tearing apart the devil's jaws. The stained glass windows from the abbey were moved to the church at nearby Stanton.

The Abbey and museum are open daily during the season of April to September (10 – 6), and from Tuesday to Sunday the rest of the year (10 – 4).

Hailes church has survived better than the abbey and is a real beauty. The wall paintings date from the 1300s and show weird beasts and monsters, the Arms of the Earl of Cornwall, and two women saints each with an adoring monk (from the abbey?) at their feet. It is a special church, often overlooked by visitors to the abbey ruins; do make time to visit.

## Didbrook

The tiny village of Didbrook is on the road to Stanway, looking down over the railway and to Dumbleton, Oxenton and Bredon hills. It has a neat and untouched church. Two cottages, nos 62 and 63, are cruck-built, which is to say that the wall and roof timbers are formed from a continuous piece of wood.

## Stanway

> *"There is in Stanway a fayre manor place and lordshipe, at the east end of the churche, a late longing to the abbay of Tweukesbyri, where he sometime lay. Mr.Tracy hathe it now in ferme".*

This was John Leland writing of his visit in the 1540s; it is little changed. The gateway was probably designed by a master-mason from Little Barrington called Timothy Strong, with its scallop shell decoration and coat of arms. The scallop was the emblem of the Tracy family who inherited the manor from Tewkesbury Abbey at the dissolution of the monasteries. The tithe barn was built in the 1300s by the Abbots of Tewkesbury. It is good to know that it is still in use almost 700 years later, being a village hall and theatre.

*Stanway*

The church of St.Peter next to the gateway forms a lovely scene. Inside the church there are several Norman parts which survived the 'restoration' of 1896 and Leland must have seen. You should also look at the War memorial in the chancel, and the grave outside to Lady Wemyss, both with wonderful lettering by Eric Gill, of Gill Sans typeface fame. It is 'Sans' as it is without serifs, the curly pieces, decorative swirls, at the end of each stroke. These examples of Gill's work are less controversial than his figure of Ariel above the entrance to Broadcasting House in London. The horrified governors ordered him to reduce the size of the male member. He did so behind a protective screen!

## G & W Railway

As you cycle back to Winchcombe you ride parallel to, and then under, the partially re-opened Gloucestershire and Warwickshire Railway. This line used to run from Cheltenham via Broadway to Honeybourne, and then on to Stratford. Let's trust that they are soon able to re-open the whole line, as forecast in many previous guides. It would be a great help in travelling around this part of the Cotswolds without a car; let's hope they allow cycles on their trains!

# 4. 'Wool, Falcons and Fish'

**Brief Description:** Incorporating an arboretum, a falconry centre, the classic Cotswold town of Chipping Campden, and its lesser known but beautiful neighbour of Broad Campden, and all within easy striking distance of Moreton-in-Marsh, this ride has something for everyone. With a lot to see it is very much a day out on cycles, rather than a challenge. If you are counting on a falconry display or other activity at Batsford, it may be wise to check in advance. I have followed this route with a party in mid-summer, setting off at 4pm. A pint in Blockley, the vision of a Little Owl out hunting over the fields, and a happy return, perfectly timed in the last of the light at around 9pm, left us all feeling we really had made the best use of this long summer evening.

**Distance**: 15 miles/24 kms – This is reduced to 9 miles/ 15 kms if you decide to miss out the Chipping Campden spur.

**Terrain**: Blockley lies over a hill, and Chipping Campden is on top of a further one, but don't let this worry you. The ascents are quite gradual and, as the ride is short, this route is possible for almost anyone, on almost any bike.

**Rail Access**: The ride starts at Moreton-in-Marsh Station on the Cotswold line. If you wished to continue west, through Chipping Campden you could cycle down the escarpment, on the B4035 and then follow the signs, reaching Honeybourne Station, on the same line in about 4 miles.

**Links With**: Two other routes are based on Moreton-in-Marsh, one going south down the Kingham valley the other heading north to Edgehill and with a link to Stratford-upon-Avon.

At Chipping Campden you are within 2 miles of Saintbury Hill on the 'Snozzle' ride from Broadway.

**Cutting It Short**: If you want to shorten the ride I'd suggest that you pause at the top of the hill with the grand view of Broad Campden and Chipping Campden ahead. Here you can decide whether you wish to cycle down to the villages and back up again to the west.

For an even more gentle and compact ride you can cycle only as far as Blockley, and then back via the arboretum. To achieve this you should simply continue ahead through Draycott, rather than turning right, to reach Blockley in half a mile.

## Route

We start from the railway station at Moreton-in-Marsh, which also has a car park.

The first part of the route is not the most direct, but does take you through lesser visited hamlets on quiet lanes.

Leave the station forecourt, passing the Post Office and turn right, with care, along the High Street. Continue over the railway and then, after 150 yards turn right (care), signed 'Todenham'. Turn left at a small crossroads (only a track to the right) after 1 mile. Continue to the A429, passing the site of the abandoned village of Lemington on your left. At the 'A' road, go left and almost immediately right (CARE). You pass through Dorn, crossing the railway, after a quarter of a mile, and then cycle on for half a mile, before turning right at a small junction. This road begins gently before climbing over Dorn Hill, reaching Draycott after 1.25 miles.

Turn left through Draycott and then turn right after 150 yards. In a quarter of a mile turn right at the B4479, and then left after only 100 yards. Continue for 1.5 miles to enter Broad Campden. Cycle through the village, passing the pub and chapel and strange topiary, and within a quarter of a mile you come to the outskirts of Chipping Campden. Turn right to visit the centre of the village.

Having explored the village, retrace your route to Broad Campden, but turn right here, by Sedgecombe House, to head for Blockley. A climb takes you to the top of the hill, and then you have a 1 mile gentle descent, steeper at the lake, passing the grounds of Northwick Park on your left. You arrive in Blockley by the church. When you have looked around Blockley, leave by the B4479, following this usually quiet 'B' road for 1 mile. Turn left at the small junction to cycle along the ridge above Batsford arboretum. After half a mile there is a right turn into the grounds which you may use with discretion; the 'No Entry' signs are to persuade cars to use a different route. Otherwise continue along the ridge, swinging right, and then turning right to arrive by the church at Batsford.

Once you have had your fill of the attractions here, return to the church and head down hill, bearing right at a small junction after 150 yards. One mile of gentle freewheeling sees you back at the High Street in Moreton-in-Marsh.

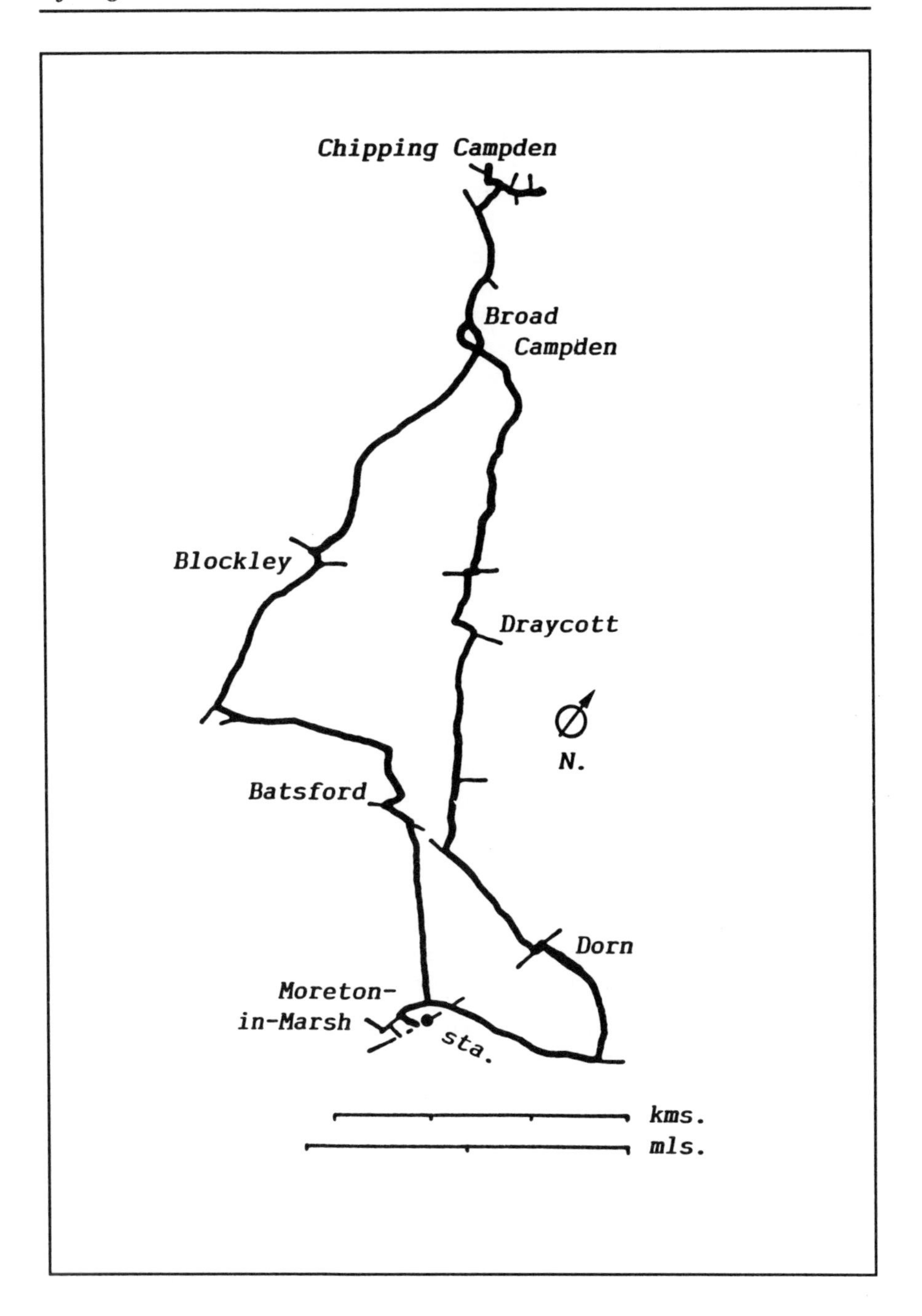
Chipping Campden
Broad
Campden
Blockley
Draycott
N.
Batsford
Dorn
Moreton-
in-Marsh
sta.
kms.
mls.

## Dorn

Though Dorn is now a tiny and unimportant hamlet, it was formerly a key crossing point and rural settlement. Camden, in his 'Brittannia', says that 'The country people have a tradition that Dorn was formerly a city, and that many old foundations that have been dug up there with an abundance of Roman and British coins commonly found by the husbandmen, and the lines in which the streets ran being still very discernible . . . show that a colony of Romans must have resided here.' Though things may not now be as 'discernible' as in 1605, you can see traces, especially when the sun is bright but low. The 10 acre site was laid out with the regular gridiron pattern associated with larger Roman towns. It was constructed close to the Fosse Way, now the A429 at this point, which ran 182 miles from Exeter to Lincoln. This must have made it an important staging post, similar in function to the coaching inns of the 18th and 19th centuries, and the service stations on todays Motorways, though with military overtones.

## Chipping Campden

For greater detail on Chipping Campden you should consult the tourist office based in the Woolstaplers Hall. Wool is easy to move while still on the sheep – the animal does the job itself. Once the wool is sheared it is extraordinarily bouncey and resilient – the product of only a few sheep takes up several cubic feet. To create the tightly packed bundles that make transport feasible, the fleeces are put in a large box with an open top. Boards are then placed on top and weight applied, usually in the form of several people. Then poles are passed through the compacted wool and the batch fastened with large staples; hence Woolstaplers Hall. The museum is also based in this building and is open daily during the 'season' of April to October. Details from 0386 840289.

The Market Hall was built by the wonderfully named Sir Baptist Hicks in 1627. It is known as the butter market, though it was reserved for the sale of cheese and poultry, as well as butter. Presumably the idea was to separate it from the wool trade. Diversification is nothing new for farmers. Sir Baptist also built the row of almshouses in the village, and a manor house. This was burnt down in the Civil War; only the gate-houses, lodges and an almonry now survive.

*Grevel House, Chipping Campden*

At a height of ten or twelve feet, on the outside walls of several buildings in the main street of Chipping Campden you will see insurance marks. These are made of metal, are about eight inches across and bear the symbol and name of the company. Each insurance company had its own fire brigade of sorts, and the mark would show which company protected each building. Being cunning operators (unlike the present day of course) the insurers had the marks made from lead; if the fire burnt the building down, the mark would melt, giving no clue as to which company had failed to protect it!

## Blockley

Blockley is a good place to stop for a while. Though prosperous, and the home of many commuters, it is still a working village. The two pubs are very different, but both welcoming. The Crown is known for its food, while the Great Western Arms is famous for commemorating the arrival of the railway.

The nearest line was the one that still runs through the Campden tunnel, opened in 1853, by the Oxford, Worcester and Wolverhampton Railway, or the 'Old Worse and Worse.' Blockley station was on this line, though nearer to Paxford. The tunnel was the site of the 'Battle of Campden' between rival gangs of workmen. When they were working on the hard and heavy construction of the line, they needed places to eat, and more importantly, drink. The 'Crown and Bell', as the Crown was then known, would have nothing to do with the workmen. The Great Western Arms was built in Blockley to serve the workmen.

The many mills that operated by the stream that runs through the village were used in the 18th and 19th centuries to for 'throwsting' (conversion of raw fibre) silk, but were gradually changed to other uses. In 1885 Lord Edward Spencer Churchill paid for the conversion of one mill to provide electric lighting for his house, the church and a shop. It is claimed that Blockley was the first village in the country to have electricity.

At the end of the High Street by the stream there is Fish Cottage. In the garden is an inscription:

*IN MEMORY*
*OF THE*
*OLD FISH.*
*UNDER THE SOIL*
*THE OLD FISH DO LIE*
*20 YEARS HE LIVED*
*AND THEN DID DIE*
*HE WAS SO TAME*
*YOU UNDERSTAND*
*HE WOULD COME AND*
*EAT OUT OF OUR HAND.*
*DIED APRIL THE 20th 1855,*
*AGED 20 YEARS.*

It's not thought that this has anything to do with the Crown Inn which now specialises in seafood!

## Batsford

Batsford Arboretum was established by Lord Redesdale when he returned from his post at the British Embassy in Japan. There are several areas which still have a Japanese feel to them. The current owner, Lord Dulverton, has continued to expand the range of species. It is worth seeing the trees at any time of year, thought the autumn colours are especially varied. The pocket handkerchief tree is spectacular earlier in the season, and won't need pointing out to you if it's in flower. Within the grounds are a garden centre (of limited interest to the cyclist unless you have very large panniers!), a tea shop, and a Falconry Centre with flying demonstrations by eagles, hawks, falcons and owls.

Details from: 0386 701043 (Falconry) or 0386 700409 (Arboretum).

# 5. 'Edgehill and a Windmill'

**Description**: This ride covers a lesser known area to the north of the Cotswolds area. To the north-west of this route is Stratford-upon-Avon which is not part of the Cotswolds, but since it is such a famous town, and so many people wish to visit it by cycle, we have shown a link to it from this ride. Stratford is one of those towns that is not easy to approach safely by cycle; our suggested access route is one of the safer and more pleasant. You will also pass the village of Edgehill with its view of the Civil War battle field and pub in a tower. Although this ride is generally flat (see 'Terrain' below) the wind can blow in quite hard. On a windy day, especially with the wind from the east, your progress may be slower.

**Distance**: 43 miles/70 kms – By taking the short cut at Tysoe and Idlicote this is reduced to 30 miles/48 kms.

**Terrain**: Generally flat from Moreton-in-Marsh as far as Tysoe but, as the name suggests, there are climbs up to Edgehill. A further flattish section then leads to some small bumps to cycle over as you return past Ilmington and Ebrington.

**Rail Access**: The ride is based on Moreton-in-Marsh station. Stratford-upon-Avon is connected by rail with Birmingham and Warwick.

**Links With**: The rides to Chipping Campden and down the Kingham valley are also centred on Moreton-in-Marsh. At Ebrington you are within 1.5 miles of Chipping Campden. At Upper Tysoe you are only three miles from Sibford Gower which is on the Whispering Knights route from Charlbury.

**Cutting It Short**: You can shorten this ride, missing out the northern section, by turning left in Tysoe to head for Oxhill. Left in Oxhill and left again having passed right through Whatcote, brings you to the nicely named Idlicote. Turn right through the village and you regain the return route at a three-way junction.

# Route

We start at the railway station in Moreton-in-Marsh, where there is also a car park.

Leave the station and go ahead, past the Post Office, to the High Street. Turn right here, with care, cycle over the railway, and then turn right (CARE) after 100 yards, signed 'Todenham'. Three miles of easy cycling, passing the Fire Service College on your right, brings you to the village of . . . Todenham! Ahead here, passing the church on your left, and the Farriers Arms, and one mile of changing views later you reach the A34. Left and immediately right at this small junction, ahead at the crossroads after 400 yards, passing Burmington, and bearing left in half a mile will bring you to Willington. Continue through the village, and half a mile later at a crossroads, just after a tiny left to the squat church at Barcheston, go ahead crossing the B4305. After half a mile there is a left turn which provides the nicest ride into and out of Shipston-on-Stour.

Otherwise continue past this left turn and you will reach another junction in half a mile, by a farm and bridge on your left. Turn right here signed St.Dennis and Tysoe. There follows four miles of very pleasant riding, with changing views all around; you should cycle ahead at the two small junctions. On your way into Upper Tysoe you have excellent views of Windmill Hill on your right.

Turn left at the first 'T' junction in the village and then right after 100 yards into Middleton Close. If you wish to visit Middle Tysoe, go ahead instead to the church and pub; return and turn left to continue. Leaving the village by this road gives you a view straight up the climb, but it does get the climb over with quite quickly. The road becomes much less steep as you climb onto the ridge. After 1 mile you turn left at the crossroads and ride almost level for 2 miles. You then reach a tricky junction with the A422. Here you need to turn right and then left after only 300 yards. The first turn is on a difficult bend, so take great CARE. Having left the 'A' road you have 1 mile of level cycling with excellent views, before reaching Edgehill, with the pub in the tower and perfect views. You can continue straight past the village, but having climbed up here it makes sense to cycle round the top of the hill through the village of Ratley. To do this turn first right at Edgehill, left at the 'T' junction in 400 yards, and left again in Ratley once you've looked around.

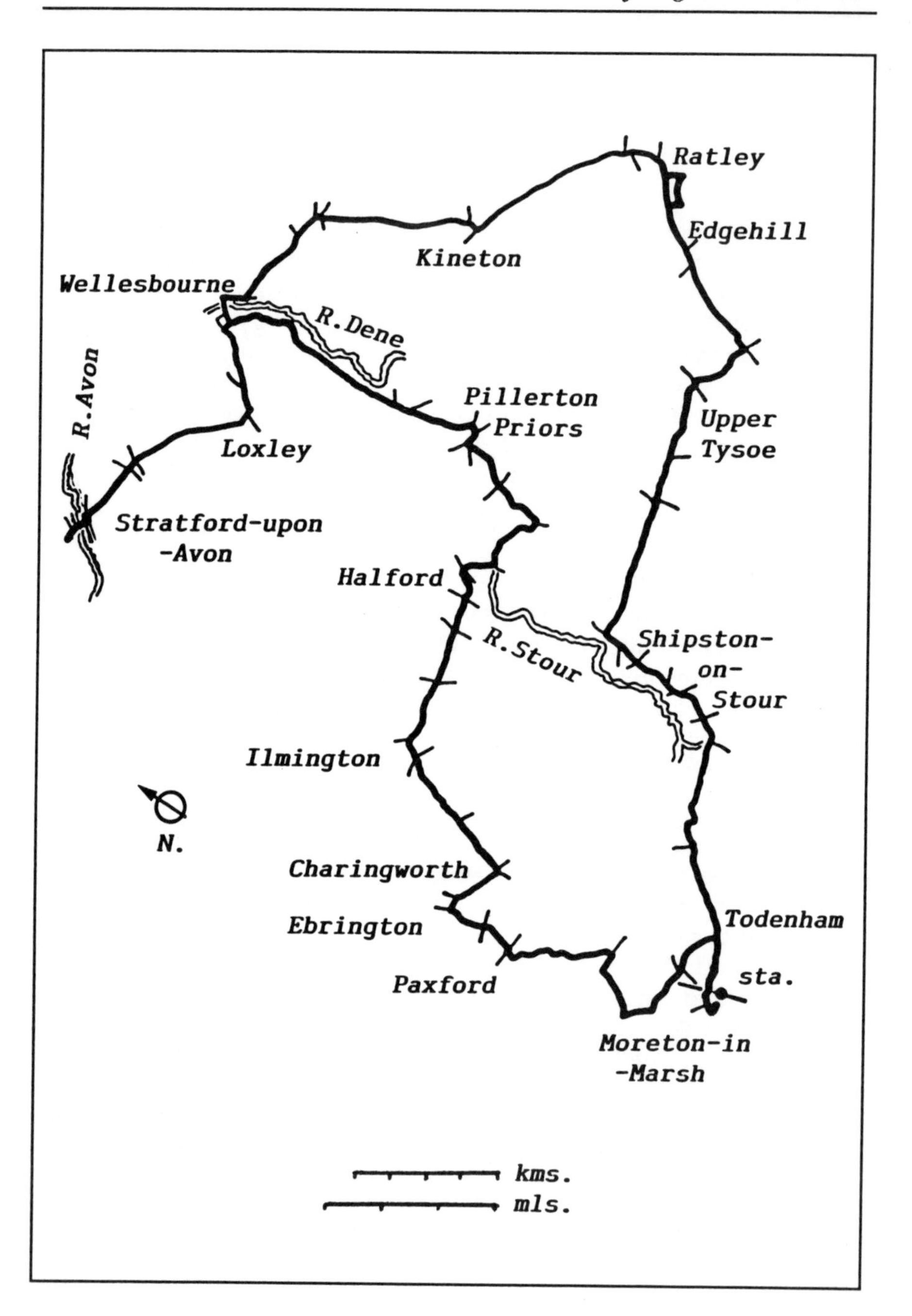
Ratley
Edgehill
Kineton
Wellesbourne
R.Dene
R.Avon
Pillerton
Priors
Upper
Tysoe
Loxley
Stratford-upon
-Avon
Halford
R.Stour
Shipston-
on-
Stour
Ilmington
N.
Charingworth
Ebrington
Todenham
sta.
Paxford
Moreton-in
-Marsh
kms.
mls.

To continue turn right along the ridge. You join the B4086 after 500 yards, bearing left down the hill, with care as it is a fast swoop. There are then 3 miles of cycling along this 'B' road, where cars can be fast, but is generally not too busy. On reaching Kineton, and having explored the town, you bear right at the three-way junction by the Swan and church, going ahead in 250 yards, when the 'B' road bears right. You cross a bridge over the disused railway, at an original metal railway sign, and then cycle on for 2.5 miles. Views to the left of a windmill base. At the five-way junction at Moreton Paddox you take the second left, which feels like straight across, with care owing to the busy Fosse Way unofficial motorway. In two miles turn right at the junction with the B4086, cycling into Wellesbourne. Wellesbourne is a mess of roads, so concentrate here!

1. To take the spur to Stratford-upon-Avon: turn left at the crossroads in the centre of the town where the B4086 crosses the B4087; continue past one major right, before bearing right onto a 300 yard section of the A429. Then, take a left turn for Loxley. Continue for 1.5 miles into Loxley, bearing right round the church and out of the village. Three miles will see you in Stratford; for the town centre turn left and then right over the Avon. Return to Wellesbourne, if you wish to, by reversing the outward route.

2. To continue on the main route back to Moreton-in-Marsh: turn left in the centre of Wellesbourne at the junction of the B4086 and B4087. After crossing the river take a left turn down Chapel Street, opposite the Stag's Head pub. Follow this small road as it turns right and then left at a 'T' junction after another 200 yards. This picks up the quiet road for Walton. After 1.25 miles you pass through Walton, continuing right at the War memorial, following the River Dene. Then cycle on for another 2 miles to reach an offset junction with the Fosse Way, which you cross. One and a quarter miles later, having turned right after a quarter of a mile, you come to the B4451 in Pillerton Priors. Here you turn right, and then right again, with CARE after 300 yards onto the A422. After only 200 yards of 'A' road, turn left onto the B4451 and then immediately left again into a small lane. Go across at Fulready after 1 mile, and continue for 1 mile, passing through a ford halfway, to reach a three-way junction where you bear right.

[This is where the short cut from Tysoe rejoins the main route.]

Turn right after a winding 1 mile to reach Halford in another half a mile. At Halford you should cross the 'A429' into the rest of the village and then cycle, walk and sneak your way past the church, over the bridge across the stream and possibly over or through a gate on a track which is parallel with the 'A' road. You then turn right, away from the 'A' road. In a quarter of a mile you cross the 'A34' and continue for half a mile to Armscote. Bear left and then immediately right to leave the village, passing the Wagon Wheel Inn. Cycle on for 1 mile, across at a junction and on for another mile to Ilmington.

Turn left to cycle through the village, and then bear left, by a wooden village hall from 1933, as the main road swings right. You quickly leave the village behind, climbing for half a mile, and then continue on top of the level ridge for 2.5 miles to reach Charingworth. Here you turn right and bear right, not down into the valley, passing the manor house, and in 1 mile reach Ebrington. At the 'T' junction, with three trees in the road, and church and manor ahead, turn left by the pub. One mile later you reach the B4479, having already crossed the B4035. Turn right to follow the 'B' road into Paxford. Leave by taking a small left, before the old shop sign as the main road bears right.

If you come out with a chapel in front of you, you have missed the turn, so go back a few yards and try again! Continue for 1.5 miles to Aston Magna. Turn right by the church, crossing the railway before turning left 50 yards later. Otherwise cycle on for 1.25 miles, through an offset junction, then turning left in front of Batsford Park and church. One and a half miles later you will re-enter Moreton-in-Marsh.

## Shipston-on-Stour

Shipston-on-Stour, the Sheepstown on the River Stour, is not an exceptional place, but it is this that makes it worth the small diversion from your route. It hasn't (yet) been invaded by the chain stores, with their identi-kit shop fronts and 'choice'. Only a little imagination is needed to take you back many decades, and picture the town as the important crossroads it once was. Several coaching inns survive around the square, the Georgian George Inn is the best preserved. Sheep Street contains several good buildings from the 1700s. Before you are carried away with images of coach and fours rattling into the town, with rosy-cheeked, colourfully dressed, coachmen blowing their horns, look at Shipston House; it was built in 1837 as the workhouse.

A year before, a railway branch line was opened to the town from Stratford-upon-Avon, replacing the tramway, which had opened 10 years earlier. You can see traces of the railway that subsequently followed its course from the bridge at Moreton-in-Marsh.

Even earlier in Shipston's history it featured in the Doomsday Book, completed in 1086. This is the entry:

*'The Church holds Shipston itself. 2 hides*
*which pay tax. In lordship 2 ploughs;*
*15 villagers and 5 smallholders with 6 ploughs. 4 male*
*slaves, 1 female.*
*A mill at 10s (shillings); meadow, 16 acres.*
*The value was and is 50s.'*

Note that the slaves are listed after the ploughs!

## Tysoe Windmill

This mill is just where you'd expect it to be, on a summit called Windmill Hill. It is in such a good position that it is built on, or near, the site of an original mill mentioned in the 1300s as being attached to the Manor of Compton Wynyates, which is at the foot of the hill to the south.

The mill you now see dates from the 1700s and has been repaired and improved many times. It used to provide the flour for the bakery in Tysoe run by Nicholas Styles; the millers at the time were Ann and Benjamin Styles, so it was a true family business. It last worked early this century, but has been fully restored.

The silhouette of a windmill is still a friendly and powerful image. The high-tech and polished wind power generators that are being studied now are creating concerns about visual pollution. Perhaps a hilltop full of even their more gentle predecessors would be overwhelming.

## Tysoe

Tysoe has three parts: Upper, Middle and Lower. According to experts in place names, Tysoe means 'a spur of land dedicated to Tiw'. This is the same God who we remember every week in 'Tuesday' and is thought to be a truly ancient pagan God. The country just to the north is known as The Vale of the Red Horse, probably referring to a hill in the red soil, by the Tiw-worshipping Hwicce tribe, who in turn gave their name to the Wychwood or Hwicce-Woda!

*Tysoe Windmill*

## Edgehill

The view from the ridge at Edgehill really is something special and worth the climb. To the east you can see as far as Ivinghoe Beacon to the north of London, while to the west the Wrekin can be spotted, to the right of the dark mass of the Welsh hills. Nearer to your view point are the Malvern Hills, Bredon and the Civil War battle site.

The battle of Edgehill took place on October 23rd. 1642 in the plain to the west of the village. The Royalist troops were spread out from Bullet Hill on the right, by the road from Kineton. The King himself was in the centre, his standard raised just by where the Round Tower is now, and the left flank was laid out along the Sun Rising. The Parliamentary forces were between Battleton (note the name), and the Kineton and Banbury road.

It was a bloody battle, in only three and a half hours 5000 men were killed or injured. Both sides claimed the victory. Cromwell however noticed the lack of skill and discipline among his Parliamentary troops, and it spurred him on to create the New Model Army.

## Kineton

Kineton used to be called Kingston, the Kings Town, and has an earthwork known as King John's Castle. What connection King John had to do with this Saxon mound we don't know, though he is buried only 35 miles away in Worcester Cathedral.

## The Next Village After Illmington

If you should get lost after leaving Illmington, don't be tempted to ask a local person the way to Ebrington: you'll get laughed at. You need to ask for directions for 'Yabberton' as this is the local pronunciation.

# 6. 'Gloucestershire Into Oxfordshire: The Valley Around Kingham'

**Brief Description**: This gentle ride has a different feel to some other routes which follow a river valley. The ridges to east and west of the Evenlode are at some distance from the stream, and are high, giving excellent views. Though it is a compact ride, the villages all have different characters and histories, often expressed through their churches.

**Distance**: 26 miles/42 kms – As an example of the several short cuts, turning for home at Kingham will reduce this to 18 miles/29 kms.

**Terrain**: There are smooth climbs up the sides of the broad valley and gentle descents. Most of the route follows the contour lines around the edge of the ridge. The track at Lower Oddington can be sticky after rain, but an alternative is described.

**Rail Access**: The ride starts and finishes at Moreton-in-Marsh station. The route also passes within a quarter of a mile of Kingham Station, the next stop down the line towards Oxford, on both the outward and return halves of the ride.

**Links With**: The ride north to Tysoe, and the Chipping Camden route are also based on Moreton-in-Marsh. At Idbury you are within 2 miles of Little Rissington on the Windrush valley ride, while at Milton-under-Wychwood you are only 3 miles from Burford and the route past Minster Lovell.

**Cutting It Short**: There are two points where you can easily curtail this ride.

The first is at Oddington, where a left turn along a a quarter of a mile of the A436 will bring you to Adlestrop on the return route. You could still take in the church at Lower Oddington on your way.

The second short cut is at Bledington, where if you continue left along the B4450 you will pass Kingham Station in a quarter of a mile and link with the return section by Kingham village. You could even take the train 'home' from here!

# Route

We start from the railway station, where there is also a car park.

Bear left out of the station and left up to the main road. Turn left over the railway bridge on the A44. After 300 yards turn right, with care, into the lane. Continue for 2 miles until you reach Evenlode. Bear right to pass the church and continue for 500 yards before turning right, across the railway and River Evenlode, to reach the village of Broadwell in under 1 mile. At the village you are by a chapel to your left; for the church you must make a short detour to your right, through the village and a ford. To continue however you should turn left for 1.5 miles to reach Lower Oddington. At the junction with the A436 turn right, with care, and then left after only 100 yards, but not into the new estate. Bear left at the first junction in the village and then right by the post office and post box to reach the church at Lower Oddington.

Once you have explored the church, if you want to avoid the track section ahead you must return to the village, turn left and follow the lane through to the B4450. Turn left here, reaching Bledington, and the main route in under 2 miles.

To continue by the track and bridle-path: continue past the church and ignore a right turn after half a mile. The surface can be rougher as the track skirts the wood, and then improves again reaching tarmac 'proper' in 1.25 miles. At the B4450 turn left through Bledington. Continue through and out of the village past the primary school on your left, and after 250 yards, as the road swings left, go straight ahead, signed Foscot and Idbury.

(For the short cut to Kingham continue on the 'B' road at this point).

Leave Bledington to cycle through the hamlets of Foscot and Bould, with their working farms, climbing gently for 1.5 miles, to reach Idbury. Circle the church on your right, turn left and left again to leave the village and head towards Fifield which you will reach in under a mile. I like the ball impaled by the top of the church spire. From here there is a mile of perfect cycling along the contour lines on the side of the ridge, followed by a climb to the junction. Turn left at the second 'crossroads', by High Lodge Farm, to descend through Milton-under-Wychwood. In the village bear left by the pub and post office, and then right at a chapel after 300 yards. A very straight mile will take you into the valley, over the river and under the railway. You then climb slightly, before turning

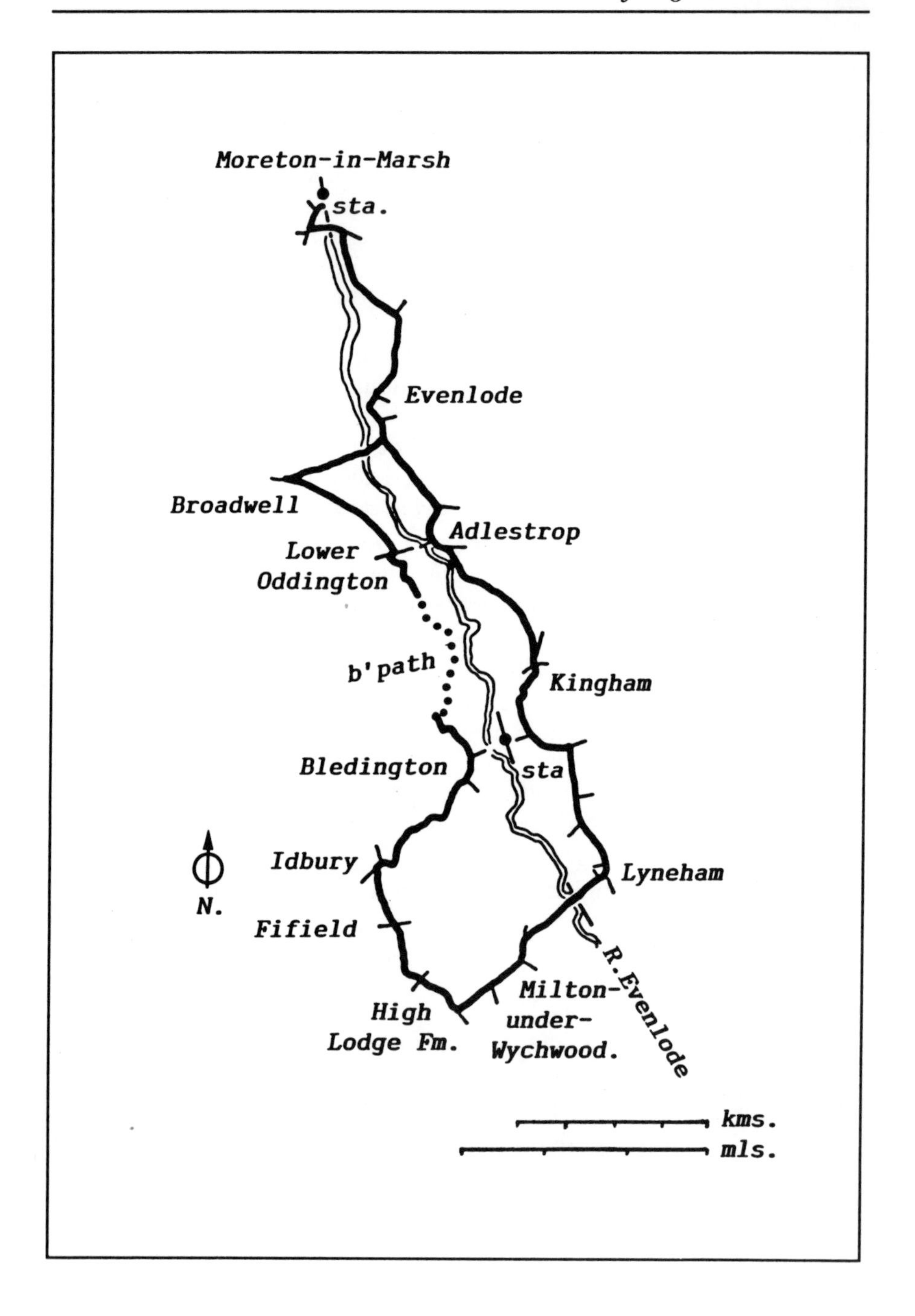
Moreton-in-Marsh
sta.
Evenlode
Broadwell
Adlestrop
Lower
Oddington
b'path
Kingham
Bledington
sta
Idbury
N.
Lyneham
Fifield
R.Evenlode
Milton-
under-
Wychwood.
High
Lodge Fm.
kms.
mls.

left round the hamlet of Lyneham. Continue for 1.5 miles to reach the B4450. Turn left for half a mile and then right (CARE) to Kingham.

Note the disused railway that you cross on your way to the village, some of which is now run as a reserve by the Woodland Trust. Wind your way through Kingham to the green and pub, cycling ahead at the junction, with the green on your right. Bear left after 300 yards and continue for a lovely mile to pass Daylesford church. At the A436 turn left, then right just before the railway line (where 'that' station used to be) skirting the grounds of Adlestrop Park. Turn left after half a mile and continue for 1.5 miles to reach Evenlode again. Leave the village and 2 miles of quiet riding will bring you back to Moreton-in-Marsh. Though this final 2 miles is covered twice the views are very different in each direction.

## Moreton-in-Marsh

Before leaving Moreton-in-Marsh, or perhaps when you return, do allow some time to look round. Despite the horribly busy main road which cuts the town in two it's a comfortable place. There are several good pubs, a bookshop with an always changing second-hand section, and a pie shop which will have your panniers bulging unless you control yourself. Wednesday the town hosts the market for the area. While the range of goods may not be as local as they once were, market day still brings in special buses from the villages all round, and there is a festive atmosphere. If you have time to explore the back lanes you'll see some fine work with Cotswold stone.

## Evenlode

Evenlode church has one of only three Sanctus chairs in the country. Most people know of the principle of churches being a place outside the law of the land, the law of the deity being the only one recognised inside the church. This is still used today; two people under threat of deportation have recently based themselves in a church. The authorities may not now be afraid of divine retribution but are still cautious of the bad publicity caused by pictures of people being dragged from a church. The Sanctus chair had to be sat in by the person seeking sanctuary. It looks worn enough to have been used many times. The church is dedicated to St.Edward, and a small piece of medieval stained glass is thought to represent his namesake, Edward the Confessor.

## Broadwell

The church is by the manor house, higher up the hill from the village, over the ford which is unusual in such an upland site. In the churchyard are several table tombs; the reason for the name will become obvious once you've seen them. Inside is a peaceful church. The Norman tympanum, originally placed over the door, is now re-set in the stairs to the tower. It shows a Maltese Cross, one with each arm of equal length as opposed to the more usual crucifix. The Knights of Malta were a powerful force in the Crusades, and this in an early example of the design which became their symbol.

## Oddington

The name of the village comes from a previous inhabitant called Odyn; the nearby stream that still runs into the Evenlode used also to be called the Odyn.

The church here was owned first by Gloucester Abbey and then handed over to York in 1157. The Archbishop of York used the village as his residence and was often visited by Henry III. It shows the power games that the church played that at least four of the churches on this short ride were administered by different Abbeys. Once established they were swapped or exchanged many times. It wasn't until the 1500s and the dissolution, that the area over which each Abbey had control became more rational.

The 'Doom' wall painting which dates from the 1300s, is still clear. Since this church was abandoned to the elements for 50 years, the paint these medieval artists used must have been of the best quality. These paintings were presumably used as a terrible warning of the consequences of a 'bad' life, or what would happen if you went against the rule of the church. The devil is seen herding wrongdoers into the mouth of hell. Heaven is a city built of bricks, rather than stone, which one writer uses to suggest that the artist came from outside the Cotswolds.

As you leave the church past the stone seats in the porch, look for the strange grooves made by local archers sharpening their arrows. Did they come to the church specially for this, or did they whet away while they were waiting for the service to begin?

## Bledington

The church at Bledington is well known for its carvings and sculptures. Most date from the 1400s when Winchcombe Abbey controlled this church and paid for a skilled team of craftsmen to work on its decoration. Their work can be seen in every corner of the building. There is also some fine stained glass dated 1476. This is thought to have been made by Richard Twygge from Malvern. I like to think of the journeys and organisation that must have been involved to arrange for Mr.Twygge to do this work.

A man, probably on horseback, perhaps on foot, travelling to Malvern to ask Twygge to look at the job. The trip to Bledington to size up the task, the gathering of the glass, lead, dyes; the draft design would have been considered by the Abbot or his deputies, revisions would be made. How did they carry glass safely by horse or cart along those rough tracks? Was the dragon in the George and the Dragon scene drawn freehand or copied from a pattern book? Stained glass is still an exacting craft with all our technical advantages; to achieve such fine results in the 1400s is even more admirable. You should also remember that few domestic buildings had glass windows. Most made use of paper, oiled to make it slightly translucent. When glass in windows did become more common they were heavily taxed. This tax lead to many blocked-in window openings; an early example of 'tax avoidance'.

## Idbury

Inside the church of St.Nicholas is another example of the church acknowledging local industry. Whereas Northleach has a brass of a sheep, and Little Rissington has a stained glass of an aircraft, Idbury has a monument to a mason. Thomas Hautin died in 1643 and his stonemason's axe and bolster (carver's hammer) are shown on the memorial plate to him and his craft. Taynton quarry, one of the most important, is only 3 miles south of here.

## Fifield

Fifield is a pretty spot on the bank of the valley, with fine views to the west. Even if you don't wish to visit the church, do notice the unusual eight-sided tower. Inside you can see a piece of stained glass showing the crown of England resting in a thorn bush, as it was supposed to have been found after the Battle of Bosworth Field in 1485.

## Kingham

Kingham Station used to be grander and more important than it is now, as the unused platforms and cast iron signs suggest. It was a junction for the line which ran from Cheltenham via Salperton, Bourton-on-the-Water and Stow, and then headed east to Chipping Norton. It used to be known as Chipping Norton junction. You can see the remains of the now disused section of line clearly to the north of the station and pass over a remaining bridge on your way to Kingham village. If this line was still used the roads in the area would certainly be safer for cycling!

*Cottages at Adlestrop*

## Adlestrop

This is the Adlestrop made famous by the Edward Thomas poem that every school child had to learn. I never did get a good definition of 'unwontedly' though it's a lovely poet's word. The remains of the station can still be seen. This was opened in 1853, but closed as part of the infamous Beeching cuts in the early 1960's.

Adlestrop Park was originally owned by Evesham Abbey, but taken over by the Leigh family in 1553. Their family name dominates the tombs and monuments in St.Mary Magdelene church in the village. Another Leigh, Theophilus, (great name – meaning 'God-loving') lived at Adlestrop House, and was visited here by his niece, Jane Austen.

# 7. 'Towards The Thames: The Lower Windrush'

Brief Description: If you begin this route from Burford (though it can easily be started from tiny Finstock station on the Cotswold line) your ride takes you by Swinbrook with its great pub and peculiar Fascist associations. The remains at Minster Lovell have their own eerie tales to tell. On leaving the Windrush valley the country changes in character, but returns to type as you pass North Leigh Roman villa and reach the Evenlode valley. Returning to the northern bank of the Windrush you pass some of the remaining Wychwood Forest, and some little visited but perfect villages.

**Distance**: 23 miles/37 kms – Joining the return route early at, say, Minster Lovell would reduce this to 11 miles/18 kms.

**Terrain**: The sections along the Evenlode and Windrush valleys are classically flat, but with enough rises to give a varied view: perfect cycling country. There is not a significant climb on this route.

**Rail Access**: The route passes Finstock Station on the Cotswold and Malvern Line. This is only a halt, and not all services stop. It is a lovely remote station and a joy to use, but you will need to check a current timetable. Every train does however call at Charlbury, only 1.5 miles from Finstock, on the B4022.

Links With: This route makes a perfect extension to the Windrush valley route based on Bourton-on-the-Water. At Finstock you are within only 1.5 miles from Charlbury and the Whispering Knights ride.

**Cutting It Short**: There are several points at which to join the return route early. These are not detailed in the route narrative, as they are clear. You can turn left at Swinbrook, Asthall or Minster Lovell to cross the Windrush.

# Route

Assuming a start from Burford (though see the comments above), we begin from the Tourist Information Centre which is off the main street.

From the Tourist Centre, go to the High Street with the museum to your right, crossing the main road and entering the slightly offset smaller road ahead. You very soon have sight of the river to your left, with rows of pollarded willows to complete the scene. Continue for 2 miles, passing the hamlet of Widford after 1 mile (which you can reach by turning left over the river) to reach the southern side of Swinbrook. At this crossroads go ahead, to reach Asthall in half a mile. Cycle through the village, to a junction where the manor, church and pub are to your left. Bear right here to reach the B4047 in under one mile.

Turn left onto the 'B' road and follow it for 1.25 miles to arrive at Minster Lovell. This section can include some fast traffic, though it is wide and has good visibility. (There is also a footpath/pavement on the left; it is illegal to cycle on this . . . !) Take the first proper left turn in the village, signed for Minster Lovell Hall, bear right and then turn left after 200 yards. Cross the River Windrush over the fine old bridge, and then turn immediately right by the Swan pub to pass the entrance to the hall

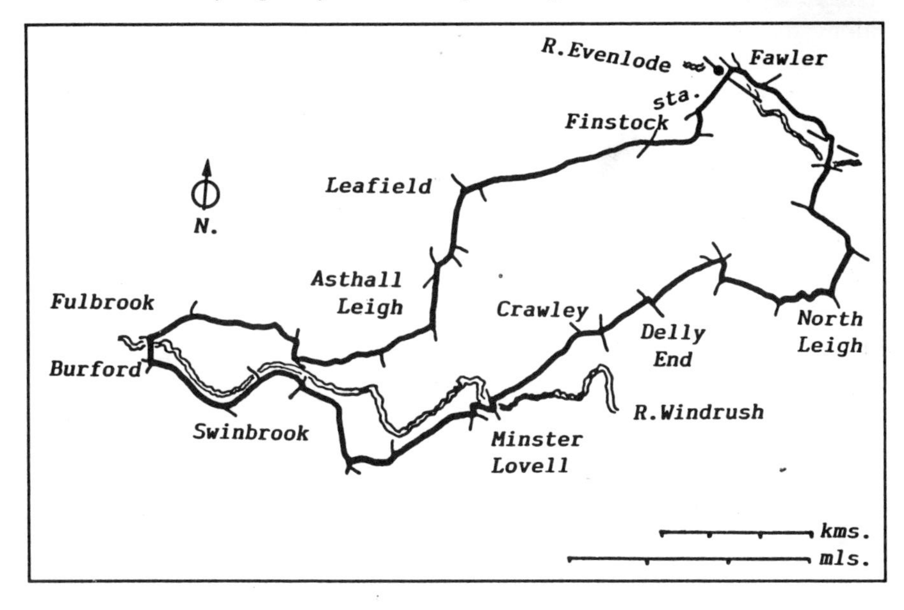

and church on your right. To visit these, go down 'Unsuitable for Motors' because you are not a motor.

To continue from Minster Lovell, bear right after 1 mile, along a good lane and left after 300 yards (continue ahead at this point for Witney, which you reach in 1.25 miles). Otherwise, continue by turning immediately right having made this turn. Continue for half a mile to the B4022 where you turn right and then first left. At the monument/shelter bear right past the village green and leave by the narrow lane. In under 1 mile turn right at an offset crossroads, and then left in 400 yards, to head for New Yatt. You reach this village after half a mile, passing the Woodman Inn, where you bear left to reach North Leigh in half a mile. Turn left in the village, into Church Road, and continue for half a mile, passing the St.Mary's on your left after a quarter of a mile. At a 'T' junction turn left, looking back for good view of North Leigh church, and ignore left after a winding half mile. Cycle on for 1 mile, through a crossroads, over the river and climb over the railway. At the small junction just over the railway turn left to ride parallel with the track for 1 mile before bearing left into Fawler. Turn left just after the tiny hamlet to pass Finstock Station.

Continue for half a mile from Finstock Station, before turning left to pass through Finstock village, bearing right at the only junction. In half a mile cross the 'B' road at the crossroads, and continue for 1.5 miles, cycling along the edge of Wychwood. You'll see the substantial church spire of Leafield from a way away. Go through the village, ignore the first left turn by the church, but bear left by the green with its two pubs and primary school, signed to Fordwells. Continue for half a mile, ignoring a small left, before taking the first right. Pass through the hamlet of Fordwells, turning left and left again, to reach Asthall Leigh in an undulating 1 mile. Continue ahead at the chapel in the village. Cycle on for 1.5 miles, along the ridge and ignoring two left turns, to arrive in Swinbrook.

The church is on the bank ahead of you, while the pub by the river is to your left. To leave the Swinbrook, turn right for 400 yards and then take the first tiny left by a cottage. A small climb leads to a further good section of ridge riding. You enter Fulbrook just over 1 mile later. There are excellent views of Burford church in the valley as you enter Fulbrook. Turn left at the A361, and then left again in half a mile, crossing the river, to re-enter Burford.

## Widford

Widford is small, cut in two by the Windrush, and the ford in the name is now replaced by a bridge. Do stop and walk to St.Oswald's church. It is set apart from the village and sits in a field, looking like an elaborate barn, with a Cotswold stone wall round it. The church was built over a Roman villa and a section of the original mosaic is still in place in the floor of the chancel. There are box pews, built to allow families to sit separately from their neighbours, and traces of wall paintings from the 1300s. This is an unspoilt place; do allow some time to stop and enjoy it.

## Minster Lovell

The gentle cluster of buildings around the ruins at Minster Lovell make a pretty scene. I like the dovecote in particular. The ruins have a strange story associated with them. Lord Lovell was on the 'wrong' side at the Battle of Bosworth in 1485, and two years later again picked the loser, fighting Lambert Simnel's cause at the Battle of Stoke. He was last seen scrambling up a river bank to escape and was presumed to have died. Rumours that he had survived continued for many years. In 1728 workmen building a new chimney discovered a chamber which contained a man seated at a table with a dog at his feet. These remains turned to dust. The story was then embellished to involve Lord Lovell's faithful servant who had been bringing him food and drink, dying and thus leaving his master to starve in his secret hiding place.

A year before the Battle of Bosworth, 1484, a rhyme featuring the Lovell family was pinned to the door of St.Paul's Cathedral in London. It read, with the spelling slightly modernised:

*'The Cat, the Rat, and Lovell our dog*
*Rule all England under an Hog'.*

Richard's emblem was a white boar, so that's the Hog; his Chancellor was William Catesby, who's the Cat; Sir Richard Ratcliffe was a close friend of Richard's, and that's the Rat, while the Lovell family emblem was a hound, which gives us the Dog! It would be a 'major' improvement if political comment was passed in such an elegant and cryptic way today.

Another Lovell legend involves the Mistletoe Chest in which a Lovell bride was suffocated, while playing hide-and-seek on her wedding day. Whom she is supposed to have been hiding from or seeking on this

*Minster Lovell*

important day we are not told. The Lovells certainly have a problem with being shut in.

## Finstock

Finstock to the west and Fawler to the east of the railway line, form one parish. The name Fawler comes from the Anglo-Saxon 'fagan floran' meaning patterned floor. With the large number of Roman settlements in the area this must refer to a mosaic. Why is the next village to the west called Stonesfield?

## The Wychwood

You pedal past the southern edge of what remains of Wychwood Forest. The Saxon tribe with their base at Cirencester were the 'Hwicca'; the 'Hwicca-Wudu' is mentioned in a charter from 841. The great trees of the forest were used for all sorts of construction. When Philip of Spain sent the Armada, assuming they would win, he especially asked them to bring back oaks from the Wychwood, with which to build the next Armada I suppose.

## Witney

To the east is the town of Witney. It is a shame that we are losing so many regional links with industries or produce; Cheddar isn't made in Cheddar anymore, the smell offended the inhabitants, and Wiltshire bacon has all but disappeared. We do still have Eccles cakes, Bath buns and Arbroath smokies that aren't simply re-creations from a large anonymous factory. Witney and blankets is another association that dates back centuries and continues today. Having the smaller rivers such as the Windrush to provide both power and clean water for washing the wool, Whitney was also ideally placed to transport the finished blankets down to London via the Thames. From London they were then sent all over the world. The North Americans would exchange more beaver pelts for a Whitney produced blanket than anything else, and they must have known, and needed their blankets.

## North Leigh

The Roman villa at North Leigh is a way to the north of the village, but our route passes within a few hundred yards of the excavations. It has two baths, Roman central heating and mosaic paintings. There is a visitor centre with very restricted opening, but the site is open 'at all reasonable times'.

## Leafield

Leafield was originally a settlement deep in the forest. This isolation led even one quite modern writer to say that the people here had a reputation for 'aggression and an uncouth dialect until recently'. With a press like that, can you be surprised?

## Swinbrook

Swinbrook churchyard includes the grave of Nancy Mitford, one of the four 'Mitford girls'. One of her books, 'Pursuit of love' was set in the manor at nearby Asthall, though she is best remembered for her distinction between 'U' and 'Non-U' ways of speaking and behaving. This itself had some unpleasant authoritarian overtones. Nancy's sister, Diana, was married to Oswald Moseley, the leader of the British fascists, or Blackshirts. A third sister, Unity was even more taken with the fascist cause and visited Hitler in Germany at the start of the war. By a bizarre coincidence, this inoffensive place in rural Oxfordshire was hit by a Nazi land mine in 1940, which blew out the east window. The remnants of the medieval stained glass were saved and are still kept in the church.

The church is also famous for its monuments to the Fettiplace family. The church is full of them, but the two sets of three reclining figures are the most interesting. One set is Tudor and the other Stuart; you can clearly see the changing fashions in hair and clothing between the two. The family had a manor house to the south of the church, but when the last Fettiplace died in 1805, this was demolished.

## Fulbrook

Though this village is rather spoilt by the barrier of the main road, it has some good features, including good solid stone cottages, which can be seen down the side streets. The churchyard contains some 'woolpack' tombs. As the name suggests they are in the shape of a bundle of wool to indicate where the occupants' wealth came from. Before you leave Fulbrook find a good place from which to view Burford High Street, across the river.

# 8. 'Old Hooky and the Whispering Knights'

**Brief Description:** Not the name of a rock band but a reference to two of the attractions on this ride, the title comes from a strong ale and an ancient monument; one may help you get the best from the other. 'Old Hooky', the ale is brewed in Hook Norton, while the Whispering Knights are one of the three Bronze Age features that make up the Rollright Stones which you pass later on the ride. Viewing the Knights, The Kings Men and the King Stone early on a misty morning is an eerie experience; a pint of Hooky may recreate the misty effect. Also featured are some classic Cotswold bridges and fords, as the route winds northwards.

**Distance:** 37 miles/60 kms – Avoiding the loop to the Sibfords will reduce this to 31 miles/50 kms.

**Terrain:** This ride has a mixture of country to cycle through. The first section that heads north, is mainly flat, and then as you bear west to the Sibfords there are several valleys that you drop into and then have to climb out of again. Leaving the Sibfords you are exposed and feel on top of the world. You maintain your height past the Rollrights before descending into Chipping Norton, and then drop into Chadlington and the Evenlode valley.

**Rail Access:** The route starts and finishes at Charlbury Station on the London-Oxford-Hereford line, also known as the Cotswold line.

**Links With:** At Charlbury you are within 1.5 miles of Finstock, which is passed by the Minster Lovell ride.

Just south of Chipping Norton you are within two miles of Kingham, which is visited by the Evenlode valley ride, based on Moreton-in-Marsh.

**Cutting It Short:** Because it is a square shaped route there are not many opportunities to shorten your ride. You can, however, turn left (west) at the crossroads just after Wigginton to follow the old railway into Hook Norton. This will avoid the northern circuit through the Sibfords. This point is indicated in the route narrative.

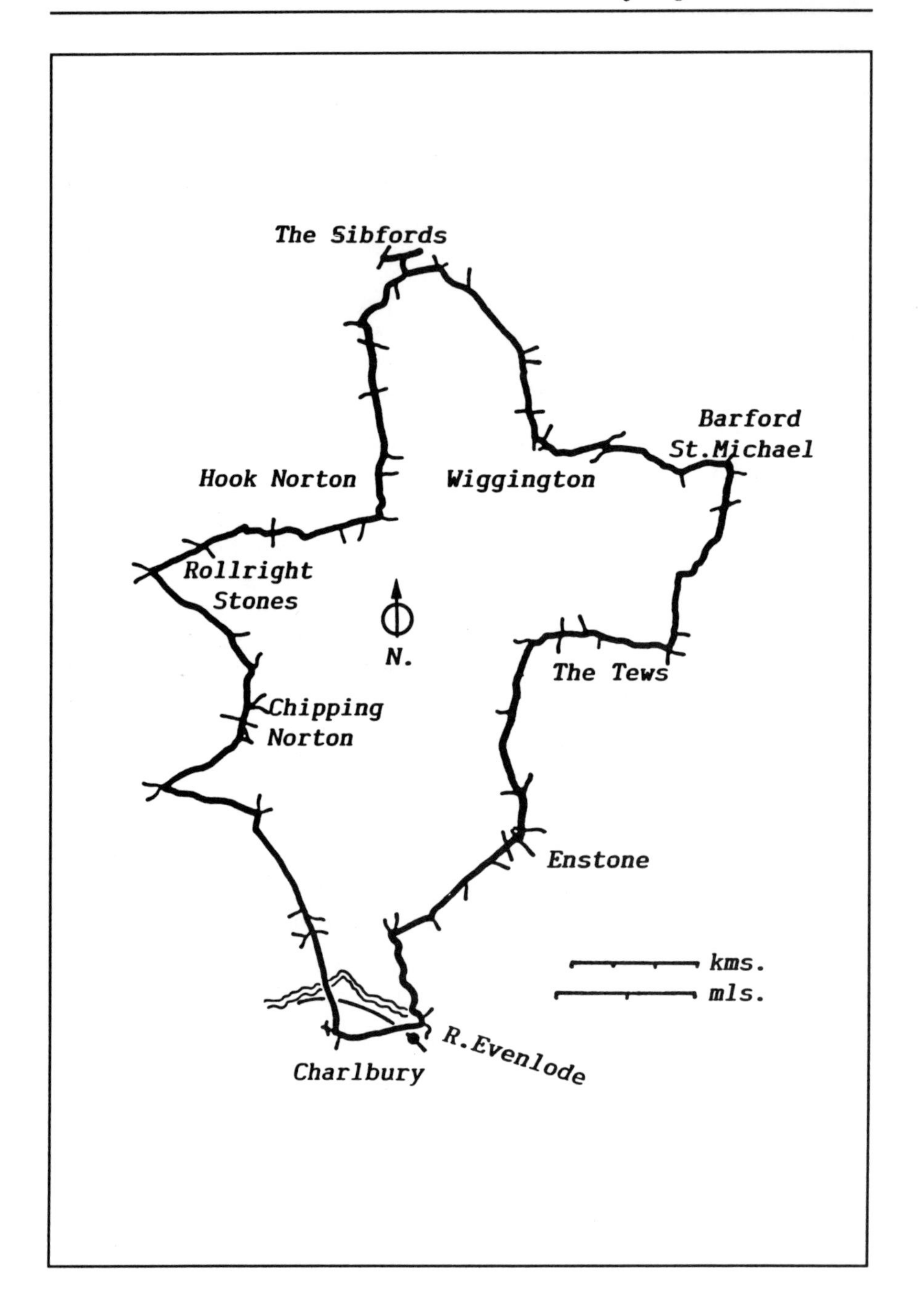
The Sibfords
Barford
St.Michael
Hook Norton
Wiggington
Rollright
Stones
N.
The Tews
Chipping
Norton
Enstone
kms.
mls.
R.Evenlode
Charlbury

# Route

We start at Charlbury station, which also has a car park. If you are starting the ride at morning commuter time beware of the streams of over-large cars arriving at the station.

Leave the station by the drive. At the tarmac turn right over the river and into the village. Turn left along the B4026 and continue for 1 mile to reach Spelsbury. Take the right (third) turn in the village and continue for 1.25 miles, passing by the hamlet of Taston on your way. When you reach the B4022, bear left onto it and follow it for just under 1 mile. Cross the A34 (it's almost a right and left) to continue on the 'B' road. Half a mile later there is another slightly offset junction at which you turn left into Enstone.

After only 100 yards turn right to have the church on your left. Having explored the church, continue ahead for 2 miles, ignoring a left turn after 1 mile, to reach Little Tew. Turn right by the church, reaching the 'B' road in less than half a mile. Go straight over, and continue for a quarter of a mile to a small left turn. Take this turn to visit Great Tew, returning by the same lane. To proceed, continue ahead at this turning passing the Park on your left, reaching a 'T' junction after 1.25 miles. Turn left here, opposite the 'No Through Road' to Ledwell, and cycle on for one mile to Nether Worton. Bear left at the village, to pass the church to your right, and continue for one mile. Cross the B4031 into the lane opposite, reaching Barford St.Michael in half a mile.

Take the first left turn in Barford St.Michael and leave the village passing the church. Turn right at a 'T' junction in half a mile, and continue for 1 mile to South Newington. The church and village are to your right; to continue, cycle up to the A361 where you turn right, with CARE. Turn left in 200 yards, to head for Wigginton which you reach after one mile. Cycle past the church to your right, and take the second right turn in the village. Continue for a quarter of a mile, to reach a crossroads.

[At this crossroads you can take the short cut to Hook Norton by turning left].

Otherwise go ahead at the this crossroads and ahead at a further crossroads in half a mile. Bear left shortly after this crossing, and continue for a lovely 1 mile. Bear left at the first junction, reaching a crossroads in half a mile. Turn left here to reach Sibford Ferris in half a mile. To visit Sibford Gower, take the right turn in the village, otherwise continue, cycling through the village, ignoring the left turn, and leave the houses behind you. Take the left turn in just over half a mile, by a stream, and continue for 2 miles, going ahead at a crossroads after 1 mile, to reach Hook Norton. You arrive in the village with the tower of the brewery to your right; to explore the other attractions, turn left, and then make your way back to this point. To continue, leave with the brewery to your right, passing a Hook Norton pub and turn first right in under 1 mile, reaching Great Rollright in a further mile. Pass the church to reach a crossroads, at which you go ahead. Bear left after half a mile, and half a mile later you reach the A34. Cross this with CARE, and in a quarter of a mile you are among the Rollright Stones.

Once you have seen, and failed to count, the stones, continue for a quarter of a mile before taking the first left. Cycle on for 1.25 miles, passing Little Rollright to your right after a short while. At the junction, having crossed the disused railway, bear right to Over Norton. Turn right at the B4026, arriving in Chipping Norton in half a mile. The town has a lot to see but is very busy with too many cars. To continue take the main 'A' road through the town, until you reach a turn for the B4450 toward, and signed for, Churchill.

After 1 mile, well before Churchill, take the first left turn. In 1.25 miles you reach the A361 where you turn right, with CARE, for 400 yards, before taking the first left turn. Two miles quite straight cycling will bring you into Chadlington. Half the village, including the church, is to your left, but your route onwards is ahead to a crossroads where you go ahead, soon leaving the village behind. After 1 mile you cross first the River Evenlode and then the railway line, reaching the B4437 in a further half mile. Turn left onto this 'B' road, and in just over one mile you'll come to Charlbury Station.

## Charlbury

Charlbury used to be a far more wooded area than it is today. It is said that Nelson's flagship, the Victory, still preserved at Portsmouth, was built from Charlbury oaks.

## Barford St. Michael

The church which gives Barford St.Michael its name has a lovely Norman doorway. It was made in about 1150, and has the classic beakhead decoration all around it, similar to some in the Windrush valley featured on other rides, and the tympanum (the piece over the door) has an interwoven figure of eight. Inside, much of the window tracery is Norman or slightly later. The builders of the church picked a fine site on the little mound, looking over the village. There are fine walls, in both brick and stone in the village.

## The Tews, Little and Great

Little and Great Tew are well known for their trimmed yew hedges. Perhaps the name comes from a corruption of Great-Yew. Both villages are lovely to cycle through providing a selection of unspoilt buildings in many styles. Great Tew provides the greatest range. The village has been administered by the estate as a closed village, allowing no incomers or second home owners in. There are a record 69 listed buildings here, many using slate from nearby Stonesfield for their roofs.

## Wiggington

Around the site of the church here, many traces of Roman buildings have been found. The largest remains were of fifteen rooms and ten mosaic floors. Some Roman bricks were even used in repairs to the tower in the 1400s. The parish records of Wigginton are well-kept, and have been used to link the life of the village and its people with that of the church. The parish used to be the authority for rates and their distribution. One example may show how illuminating these surviving records can be.

A tablet on the wall of the church, near the south door is dedicated to the Samman family. David and his wife, the sadly named Silence, had six sons and four daughters, between October 1786 and August 1807. Ten children in 21 years. They all died; none of them lived longer than seven months. The local records show that despite this sadness in his life David Samman was the largest rate-payer in the area by 1810, and a prosperous farmer. But the accounts of the 'Wigginton Overseers of the

Poor' show that less than ten years later he was receiving the forerunner of social security, 'parish relief'. He was officially a pauper.

## The Sibfords

Sibford Ferris and Sibford Gower are on either side of a stream. The ford was named after Sibba, an Anglo-Saxon; the land to the north was owned by Thomas Guher, the land to the south by the Ferrers family, which explains the second half of the names. This was Quaker country, and a large school building still exists at Sibford Ferris and a Friends meeting house at Sibford Gower.

## Hook Norton

Hook Norton was originally called Hog's Norton. 'Where the pigs play the organ' went the rhyme, which defined inhabitants of the village as exceptionally rude and bad mannered. Perhaps the name was altered to change this unfortunate image.

Do visit St.Peters church in Hook Norton, even if you only examine the font. This is Norman and shows Adam and Eve, with some signs of the Zodiac, including Sagittarius. This blend of Christian and more mystical symbols was not unusual, but the 'pagan' ones were often later removed or destroyed. In Worcester Cathedral, for example, a tiled mosaic of the complete astrological signs is still covered with a carefully placed carpet!

The brewery remains as a substantial, working building, while previous industries have only left their mark. The pillars which supported the railway line are still standing. The cutting to the south of the village is cared for by the local naturalist trust and you can visit this unusual nature reserve. The railway was essential for Hook Norton's iron industry, carrying the ore to South Wales for processing. As often happens the creation of services for one industry enables others to prosper. The nearby village of Shutford became a centre for the manufacture of 'plush' before the railway came, but was able to survive until 1948 because of the good transport. Plush was a woolly, open weave velvet, first used for ornamental horse trimmings, became popular with the Victorians for internal decoration. It was apparently difficult to persuade the skilled workers from the towns to come and work in such a quiet and out of the way place. We still of course use the word plush to describe something soft and opulent looking.

*Whispering Knights*

## The Rollright Stones

As long as you don't expect as large or dramatic a structure as, say, Stonehenge this spot is still special. The Rollright Stones, the Whispering Knights, the Kings Men and the King Stone are all part of one monument, though they were altered and added to for many centuries. When originally constructed in around 1700BC, there were only eleven stones in the circle. The site was chosen since it straddled the ancient tracks which ran from north of Edgehill all the way to Bath.

The Knights were first constructed as a barrow, but when this collapsed, and the soil was washed away, it formed the collection of stones which does look like a group of men, huddled together, perhaps whispering to each other. The stone that leans most, trying to catch every word, used to be the roof stone.

The King's Men form the circle, around 100ft in diameter, and there are about 70 of them. The legend associated with them says they cannot be counted, perhaps moving or hiding when they are out of your sight. Why not try it? A baker is supposed to have done so several centuries ago, trying to beat the legend by putting a loaf on each stone. When he returned to his start point, the first loaves had disappeared. One source suggests this is an ancient folk memory, associating the stones with offerings to produce a good harvest. Try scattering some crumbs from your sandwiches; you never know . . .

The King Stone is now cut off from the circle by the road, but is aligned with the circle, and seems to be placed with reference to the sunrise and sunset.

## Chadlington

Chadlington is a long village running along both sides of the road for over a mile. The first section is rather bleak. To distinguish its different parts there are a Millend, Brookend and Greenend, as well as the more standard Eastend and Westend. It has a large manor house; you can see the substantial chimneys over the hedge, as you cycle past. There are good views here, which must have been one reason why the Vikings and earlier settlers chose the area around the village for their camps.

# 9. 'Bosworth Flag, and Tenpenny Nails to Eat'

**Brief Description:** Best described as a swoop around the Thames valley, this route gives you an opportunity to catch up with the water that you've seen flowing under, or even over, your wheels while following rides further upstream. The Windrush, the Leach, the Coln, the Cole and other streams all join the Isis as it is known at this point, just before it becomes the Thames 'proper'. You may see some Morris dancing (not may see Morris dancing, that joke is out) at Bampton. Also worth pausing for is the Bosworth flag at Stanton Harcourt, Roman remains and some quiet villages. The roads are quiet once you leave the outskirts of Oxford.

**Distance:** 34 miles/55 kms – If you use the ford crossing; 39 miles/63 kms by way of the road.

**Terrain:** There are no hills on this ride; you are in the 'Oxfordshire Plain'. The cycling is easy. Being in a plain, however, the wind can blow strongly, with little to shelter you, and this can have the same effect on your progress as climbing a hill. The traffic nearer Oxford can be busy, but this city is used to lots of cyclists and often provides cycle tracks or paths.

**Rail Access:** The ride is based at Oxford Station, which is on many lines – north, south, east and west, including Inter-City routes, as well as being at the eastern end of the Cotswold and Malvern Line. Charlbury Station is 9 miles of Bampton on this line.

**Links With:** Apart from the first section of the linear ride from Oxford to Bath, which uses the same start from Oxford, at Bampton you arer within 5 miles of Minster Lovell, on the route eastwards from Burford.

**Cutting It Short:** There is no opportunity to shorten this ride once you've begun to follow the river, due to the lack of bridges.

## Route

NOTE: This ride features two different crossings of the Thames. One uses the Tadpole bridge on a tarmac road; the other crosses by way of the hamlets of Duxford and Chimney, using a ford and tiny bridge.

The Tadpole bridge can be used all year round. But the ford can be quite deep and wide. The woman who lives by the ford, and must know it better than anyone, says that it is a fine crossing for cycles in June, July and August, or any other time when there has been little rain. I don't mind wading, but if you do, stick to the drier months for exploring this special and ancient way across the Thames.

We start at Oxford station which also has a car park, and parking for about 1000 cycles!

This first section follows the same route as the Oxfordshire Cycleway; you'll see the small blue signs to help you find your way.

Cycle out of the station forecourt to the main road. Turn right with CARE, to cycle under the railway. Continue for 1 mile to a busy junction where the A420 bears right. Go ahead at this point along the B4044, cycling under the 'A420' and then bearing left after a quarter of a mile up Cumnor Hill. Continue for 1.25 miles to cross over the dual-carriageway, pass the church at Cumnor before turning left to Appleton.

You have now escaped the clutches of the Oxford suburbs. Continue for 1 mile before turning first right, and then left after 100 yards (the hamlet of Eaton, pub and 'phone box lies ahead before this left). Continue for 1 mile to reach Appleton. Go ahead through the village, passing the church and manor on your left, before leaving by bearing right. Cycle ahead for 2.5 miles to reach the A415. Go straight across, with care, and continue, passing Longworth for 1.5 miles to reach Hinton Waldrist on your right. I'd suggest that you visit the village whichever Thames crossing you chose.

For the Chimney ford Thames crossing, proceed as follows:

Cycle through the village of Hinton Waldrist, past the church, and on for half a mile to the hamlet of Duxford. As the track swings left, turn right to take a track to the ford, which you reach in only 50 yards. Cross the ford with care and go through the trees, and continue along the track to cross water again in just over a quarter of a mile. Cycle on once you have crossed the river, into the hamlet of Chimney. Follow the lane for 1.5 miles to reach Aston. [If you wish to take in Bampton, despite using the ford crossing, you can do so by turning left, by a bridge, halfway along this lane; turn right in 1 mile, reaching Bampton 1.5 miles later].

To continue, using the Tadpole Bridge crossing:

Continue ahead at Hinton Waldrist, leaving the village to your right. After 1 mile you reach the A420, where you turn right, with CARE, for only 50 yards, before turning left onto the B4508. Continue for 1.5 miles,

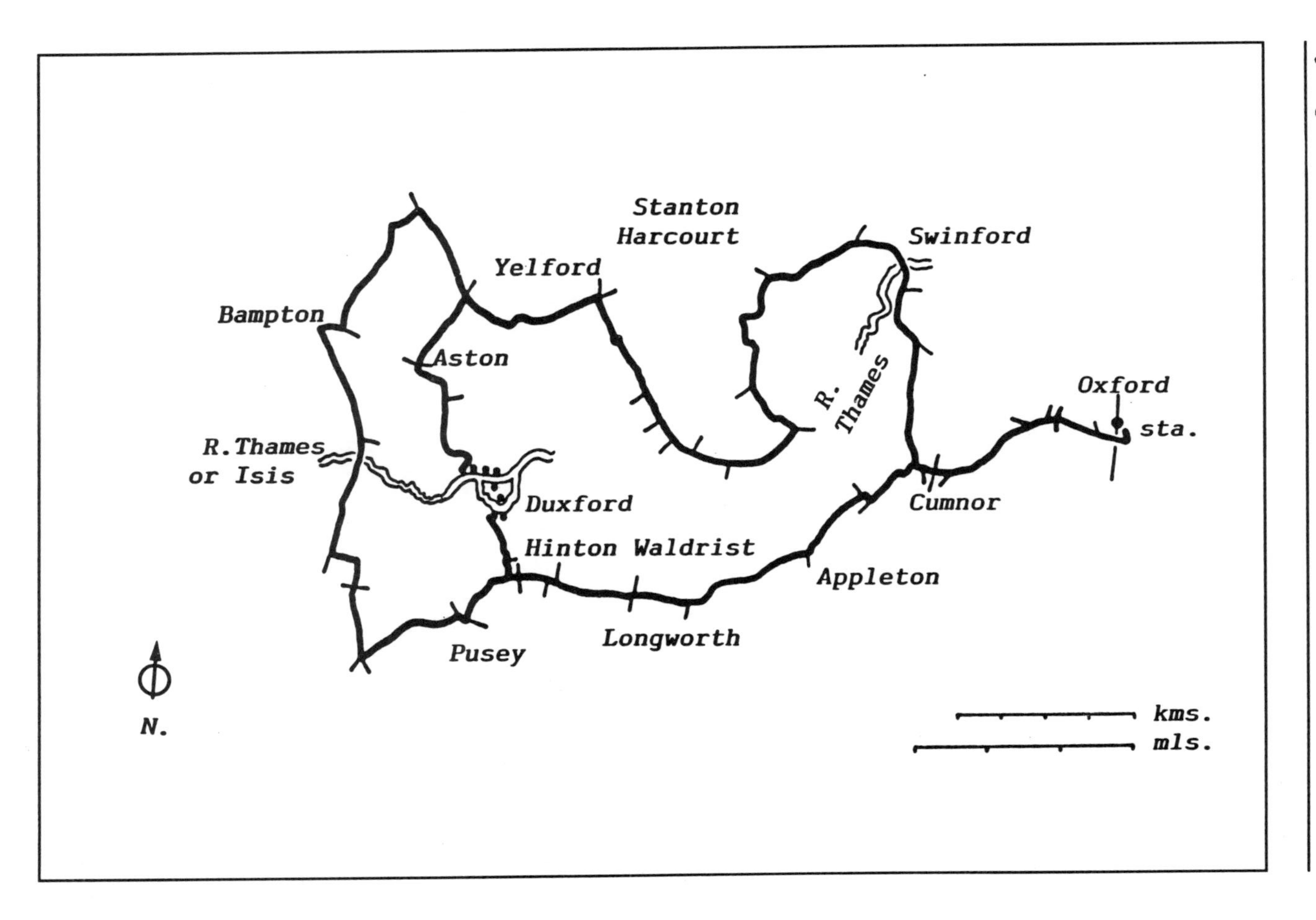
Stanton
Harcourt
Swinford
Yelford
Bampton
Aston
R.
Thames
Oxford
sta.
R.Thames
or Isis
Duxford
Cumnor
Hinton Waldrist
Appleton
Longworth
Pusey
N.
kms.
mls.

passing and perhaps visiting Pusey on the way. At the first crossroads turn right, and continue for 1 mile to meet the A420 again. Go straight across here to reach the village of Buckland in a quarter of a mile. Continue through the village, and take the first major left turn, with the college and church ahead of you. Cycle on for a quarter of a mile, past the front of the college to a 'T' junction. Turn right here and continue for 3 miles, crossing Tadpole Bridge and a pub, at about halfway, to arrive in Bampton. The church, shops, and pubs are in the village centre to your left. To continue, you turn right for 300 yards, before taking the first left. In just over 1.5 flat miles you reach the first junction, at which you turn right. In 1.25 miles you come to a crossroads.

At this crossroads you turn right if you have come via Aston or continue ahead if you have cycled through Bampton.

Continue for 1 mile, passing through the very quiet village of Yelford, to reach a crossroads, with tracks to left and right. Turn right, and continue for a straight 1 mile, to reach the A415. Turn right here, with CARE, bearing left after 150 yards, and continuing for a quarter of a mile, before turning left by a 'phone box. Turn right in half a mile. Pass the church on your left as you enter Standlake, and continue for half a mile. Ignore two left turns, before cycling straight ahead as the 'B' road turns firmly left, reaching Northmoor in under 1 mile. Pass the church and pub, and leave the village behind, arriving at a small 'T' junction in half a mile. Just to your right here is a pub by the river, and it was until recently the site of a passenger ferry across the Thames. Lets hope it can re-start.

To continue, turn left at this junction, and in 1 mile turn right to reach Stanton Harcourt half a mile later. Do explore the village, but once you have leave it by staying on the main through road, the B4449 to reach a (completely unnecessary) roundabout in 400 yards. Take the second exit, effectively turning right, to reach Sutton in a quarter of a mile. Continue for 1.5 miles to reach the first junction. Turn half right here, along the 'B4044', to another strangely sited roundabout. Take the third exit, effectively straight on, reaching the bridge over the Thames at Swinford in 400 yards.

Having crossed the river, continue for 1.25 miles, before turning right, with care, at Farmoor onto the B4017. Continue, passing Farmoor reservoir on your right, for 1.5 miles, where you join your outward route by Cumnor church. Bear left to follow the (blue signed) route back to Oxford Station.

## Hinton Waldrist

At Hinton Waldrist there is a well preserved toll-house, with a thatched roof and rounded front. This last feature was perhaps to give good visibility, to watch for approaching coaches. Only rich people could afford a fast coach and two, or four. The rest had to share their journey with goods:

"The London waggon . . . was drawn by eight strong horses. It had very broad wheels. A large punt, or square shaped boat was suspended by chains to the bottom of the waggon between the wheels. In this punt lambs, sheep, pigs and poultry of various sorts were carried, being fed at intervals on the journey. In the bed of the waggon goods of a heavy character were packed three or four in height, on the top of these were five or six tiers consisting of butter in flats, and carcasses of sheep and pigs. The size of the waggon was 18 feet in length, $7^1/_2$ feet in breadth at the bottom of the waggon and 12 feet to the top of the tilt . . . A light ladder to reach the top of the load was securely placed at the side of the waggon . . . Two waggoners, with massive whips, always travelled with the team" wrote Thomas Ward Boss in his 'Reminiscences of Old Banbury'.

The thought of machines such as this travelling the rough roads and even using the ford at Chimney, is extraordinary. The keen ambition of many smaller towns and villages to be connected to the railway network is very understandable.

## Bampton

Bampton is known as one of the best recorded schools of Morris dancing. Each area has its own style of tunes and steps. Whereas most teams dancing now have restarted a tradition which has faded, Bampton Morris claims to have a continuous heritage, except for the years of the First World War. An extra member of the team here carries a cake impaled on a sword; the cake is cut into pieces and sold to the crowd, and is meant to bring fertility to women who eat it.

With the abundant sheep skins and the deer from the nearby estates and the Wychwood, Bampton became one of the centres of the glove making industry. The work could be carried out at home, and all the year round. The men used their strength for the stretching of the skins, the women did the cutting and basic stitching, while the children used their tiny fingers to sew the end of the fingers of the gloves. It must have been hard work for little money, like the outworkers and pieceworkers of today. The prosperity that this industry brought to the landowners of Bampton can be seen in several fine houses, not in the homes of the workers who produced the gloves.

*Pope's Tower, Stanton Harcourt*

## Yelford

Yelford is a lovely place, very quiet and unspoilt. It has only a church, a manor house and three other houses. Next to the church, dedicated to St.Nicholas and St.Swithun, the manor sits on a raised piece of land and has a moat round it. The two wings of the hall are clearly different, one provided the servants' quarters, the other was the 'solar' wing. It is timber framed, but on stone foundations and footings.

## Stanton Harcourt

The Manor House at Stanton Harcourt was demolished in the 1750's (the dismantled stone being taken down the Thames by barge to build Lord Harcourts new house at Nuneham Courtenay) but the kitchen and some other pieces remain. Forget any idea of an average kitchen, or even a simply larger version of one you may remember from Hollywood films of medieval England. It is without a chimney, and had rows of shutters which could be opened or closed to suit the wind direction. Despite these vents, with smoke and fumes from two fires and three ovens, it must have been an unbearable place in which to cook.

Alexander Pope, who stayed here in 1717-8 while translating the 'Iliad', described the kitchen: "The horror of it has made such an impression upon the country people, that they believe the witches keep their Sabbath here, and that once a year the Devil treats them with infernal venison, viz. a toasted tiger stuffed with tenpenny nails". Before you leave the kitchen, perhaps you can't stand the heat, do look up, or better still lie down, and admire the roof built in 1485, and like a spider's web.

To the east of the church is the parsonage, next to which is a row of medieval fish ponds. These were used much as we use a present-day refrigerator, to store fish until they were to be eaten. While they were stored they grew; an advantage over the modern 'fridge.

The church has so much of interest even on a swift visit that I'll only single out one piece which is both history and literature. Robert Harcourt was standard bearer to Henry VII. At the Battle of Bosworth Field in 1485 his master defeated Richard III to become King. This was the encounter at which Shakespeare has Richard offering his kingdom for a horse. The flag, or standard, carried by Robert Harcourt at the battle was presented to him in acknowledgement of his service, and still hangs in the church, above his tomb.

# 10. 'Classic Cotswolds: The Upper Windrush Valley'

**Brief Description:** The River Windrush links with the Thames on its way to the sea. This lucky confluence was used to transport the honey coloured, and easy-to-work, Cotswold stone from the neighbouring quarries to London to build such famous structures as St.Paul's cathedral. Being along a valley for much of the route, you should find your way with ease and the lanes are perfect for cycling. It comes as a shock when you pop out into Burford with its noise and traffic, but don't be tempted to leave Burford too quickly – the church with its wide range of associations and 1900 years of history is an essential visit. You have fine views of the valley that links Bourton-on-the-Water with the Windrush. As you cycle onto the ridge by Clapton you can clearly see across to the Rissingtons which you pass later on the ride. This valley is an unusual feature, as it does not have a road running along the course of the stream.

**Distance:** 21 miles/34 kms – Crossing the river to return at the Barringtons reduces this to 14 miles/22 kms.

**Terrain:** There is a climb out of Bourton-on-the-Water, as you might expect to reach a place called Clapton-on-the-Hill, but this is followed by a glorious descent into the Windrush valley by Sherbourne. You then have some classic, flat, valley cycling to reach Burford. A gentle rise leads you to Taynton, and on to Great Barrington. The long-ish but gentle climb to Little Rissington is accompanied by good views and interesting flowers and wildlife, to take your mind off the incline. The final 'whoosh' into Bourton speeds up in places, so take care.

**Rail Access:** The nearest station is Shipton, with only a partial service, 3 miles from Burford. Kingham Station which has a full stopping service is 6 miles from Bourton-on-the-Water.

**Links With:** The most obvious and excellent link is with the Minster Lovell ride which can be incorporated by continuing along the Windrush valley at Burford. This creates a figure-of-eight ride with Burford at its centre. Three other routes, to Chedworth, the Slaughters and the 'Hell' ride, are all based on Bourton-on-the-Water.

**Cutting It Short**: You can begin your return early by turning left to cross the Windrush just before Little Barrington to join the route at Great Barrington. This misses out the gentle section to Burford, so it may cut down on time, but not on effort.

# Route

We start at the town end of the greens and bridges in Bourton-on-the-Water, by the cafe and museum.

Cross the tiny bridge with the museum on your right, up a lane passing a coffee shop. The hill becomes steep quite soon and continues for half a mile. Ignore the small sharp right turn, and carry on for 1 mile. Turn left

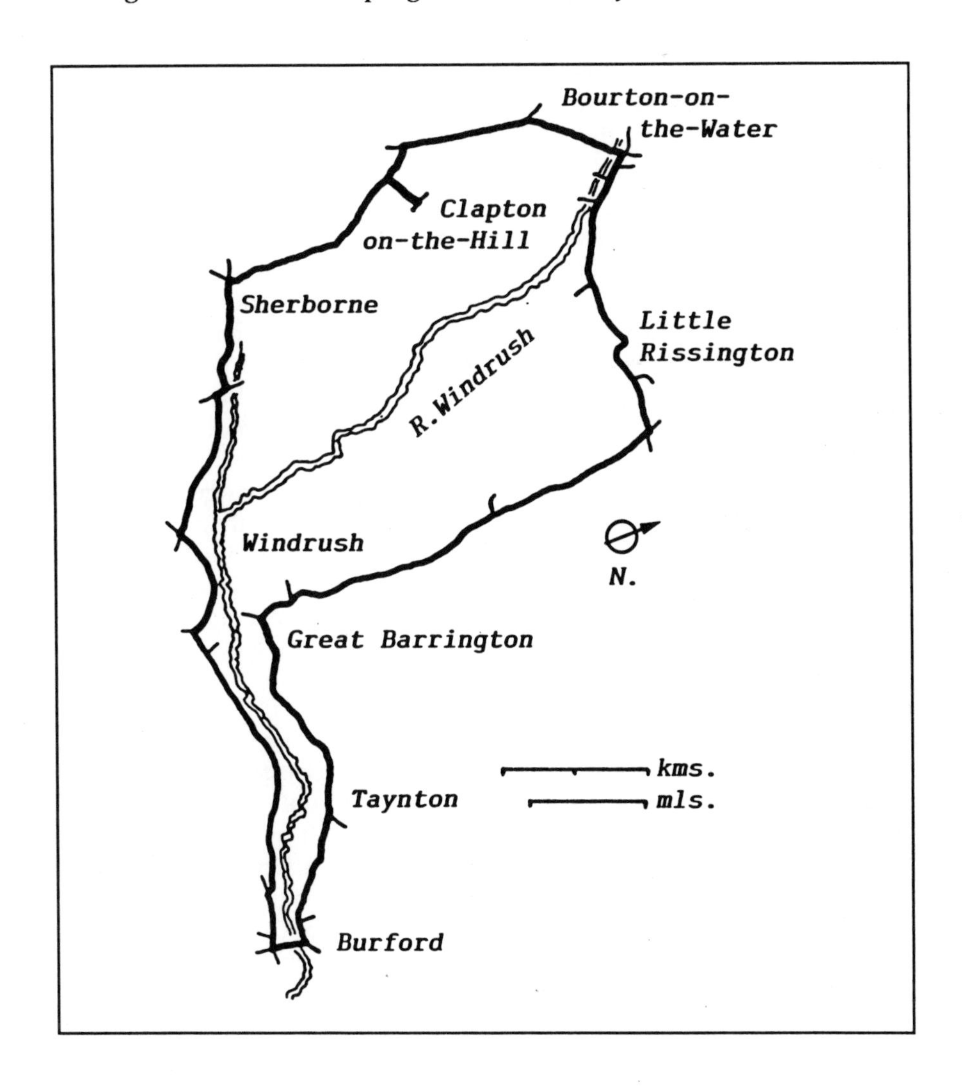

at three-way junction and cycle on to another turn after 400 yards. Here you can either continue ahead, or to visit Clapton-on-the-Hill turn left and return. Continue smoothly downhill for 2 miles, into the Sherbourne Valley. Cross the brook and then turn right. Pass the park on your right, followed by the church. After 1 mile at a 'T', turn right and then swing left. One mile onwards you come into Windrush. To continue, turn left by the church. You have sight of the River Windrush on your left for 1 mile before reaching Little Barrington.

Don't take the left by The Fox, but wait a few hundred yards before taking a tiny left turn. Pass the church on your left as you leave the village, before enjoying two miles of perfect valley cycling. Turn left, opposite the church, at the B4425, and after half a mile you come to Burford.

After exploring the town, leave by going downhill to the bridge, while attempting to avoid the cars, (the excellent church is on your right, near the river), cross the river and then turn left on the 'A' road. After 200 yards go ahead into the lane, thankfully leaving the traffic behind, and continue for 1 mile to reach Taynton. Passing the church on your left, continue through the village and 1 mile later you will come to Great Barrington. After the village, at the 'T' junction, with the park ahead, turn right. This is a slow and gentle, but quite long climb, which you can mitigate by enjoying the view. After 2 miles you either turn left into Great Rissington past the pub. OR continue along the ridge for 1 mile, before turning left above Little Rissington instead. Both give obvious descents back into the valley. Turn left at the junction, in the valley if you have come by way of Great Rissington, ahead if you have come through Little Rissington, to re-enter Bourton-on-the-Water, avoiding the fast cars, coaches and suicidal pedestrians if you can!

## Clapton-On-The-Hill

The church at Clapton-on-the-Hill is one of the smallest in the area, measuring only 30 feet by 13 feet at the nave and only 15 feet by 11 feet at the chancel. It dates from 1200, is mainly unspoilt by 'restoration', and a lovely spot to spend a quiet few minutes. The inscription on the north side of the chancel arch is of interest to experts in such things. It describes how anyone who says an Our Father and a Hail Mary three times while 'devoutly kneeling', will be rewarded with a thousand days. Presumably an extra thousand days' life was intended to be an incentive even in times when life was very hard. It would also give the recipient a further chance to kneel and pray and perhaps 'win' a further extension!

## Sherbourne

Sherbourne village has a several unusual features. The church of St.Mary Magdelane is joined at its south east corner by a corridor to the adjacent 14th century manor house. The small cottage standing apart in the grounds of the house was originally built as a grandstand from which the local nobility and their guests could watch deer coursing with greyhounds. As you pedal through keep an eye out for number 88, another cottage that wasn't originally designed to be one. This was a Norman church and, once you know this, you can pick out some clearly church-like features.

## Windrush

St.Peter's church at Windrush is famous for its Norman doorway, so you don't even have to enter the church to appreciate the delicate and fresh work with stone. The beakheads fix you with their stares from all around. If you do go into the church you'll enjoy more Norman features. When a Royal Commission was investigating possible building materials for the new Houses of Parliament in 1839, they were shown Windrush church to demonstrate how well the local stone lasted.

## Burford

As an example of how churches can illuminate the social, cultural and political life of a community, the church at Burford is perfect.

Cromwell had won the war against the tyranny of the monarchy. The predominance of parliament as the means of government had been established. Many of the troops who had supported Cromwell in the bloody war wanted to take the opportunity to make more profound and fundamental changes to society; Cromwell however began to display the same autocratic tendencies as the monarch he had replaced.

The Levellers, as the more radical group were known, wanting a more level society, were condemned by Cromwell. At Burford Cromwell and Fairfax caught up with a group of them and after a skirmish at the corner of Sheep Street, a group of 340 was held prisoner in the church.

Three were shot and buried four days later on May 19th, 1649. The last to be shot, John Church, "Stretched out his arms, and bade the soldiers do their duty, looking them in the face, till they gave fire upon him, without the least kind of fear or terror". One of their colleagues, also held, was forced to watch the execution. He scratched 'Anthony Sedley Prisner' on the rim of the font. This inscription is still there for you to see. Another man, one of the ringleaders called Cornet Denne, was taken out to be shot with the others, but was then reprieved at the last moment. In return he was forced to tell his fellow Levellers what a fine man Cromwell was. A leaflet produced by the surviving Levellers attacked Cornet Denne for his treachery: "howling and weeping like a crocodile, and to make him a perfect rogue and villain upon everlasting record".

Having been dismissed as an aftermath of the Civil War, or 'a footnote in history' for many years, modern writers such as Tony Benn now see the Levellers as early socialists. With their theme of the Earth being a 'common treasury' for all man kind they can also be accepted as the first environmentalists. A plaque has been erected to the three Levellers who were shot, on the wall of the church.

## Taynton

The Romans made coffins from Taynton stone, and the quarries here were recorded as one of the village's assets in the Doomsday Book.

Merton Tower in Oxford was constructed from Taynton stone as early as 1310. It was not only the free cutting quality of the stone itself (hence the term 'freestone') that made it attractive. There were no vans, cranes, railways in the 1300s; even the carts must have been primitive. At Taynton the masons had 'only' to roll, drag and push the blocks of stone down the hill to the Windrush. It could then be loaded onto barges and the current would provide most of the power to transport the stone to Oxford. Traces of a slipway, and the sluices to raise the water level to float the barges, can be seen near Little Barrington.

Further down the Thames are Eton and London. Taynton stone is found in Eton chapel. Stonemasons from the village came across their local material in the ruins when they were employed to rebuild St.Paul's after the Great Fire of London.

*Cottages at Taynton*

Though we think Cotswold stone is Cotswold stone, each type has its own qualities and purposes. Taynton stone is one of the best as it does not suffer from 'onion weathering'. Look closely at some Cotswold stone buildings and you will sometimes see the layered, flaky rings which this describes. Taynton stone can also be cut extremely thin; it can be used as a veneer or facing. The New Bodleian Library in Oxford is a good example of this technique.

## Little Rissington

The village is just downhill from the airfield. Inside the church, which dates from the 1100s, there are monuments to fliers who died while training at the R.A.F..F. Central Flying School, which was based at the airfield. There is even a stained glass window which, against a roundel of blue, portrays a bright red training aircraft of the type used at the airfield. If this seems incongruous in a religious building, remember it is only a modern version of the tradition of acknowledging the local crafts and activities which bring prosperity to a community.

# 11. 'A Coupla Swells and Slaughters'

**Brief Description:** Another odd name for a cycle ride, the Slaughters and Swells each with an Upper and Lower, are among the most photographed villages in the area. With their tiny lanes, small bridges and neat fords, they are ideal for exploring by bicycle. This short ride, based on Bourton-on-the-Water, also passes close to Stow-on-the-Wold from where you could easily join the route if you wished.

The route includes a pedal by Donnington brewery, which is so beautiful and perfectly sited, that it would produce a smacking of the lips even in the most vehement tee-totaller. As you can't buy beer at the site, we pass a couple of pubs that stock their local beer later in the itinerary.

**Distance:** 14 miles/23 kms – If you only visit the Slaughters, this is reduced to 8 miles/13 kms.

**Terrain:** This is a short and gentle ride. There are some small climbs as you skirt the hill around Stow-on-the-Wold, but none are sharp or long.

**Rail Access:** The nearest station to Bourton-on-the-Water is Kingham, 6 miles away. At Donnington brewery you are within 4 miles of Moreton-in-Marsh station, via Longborough and the A429.

**Links With:** The Windrush valley, Chedworth and the partly off-road 'Hell' routes are all also based at Bourton-on-the-Water. Broadwell, on the Kingham valley ride, is within 2 miles of Upper Swell via Donnington.

**Cutting It Short:** To create a very short excursion, only taking in the Slaughters, you can simply turn left onto the B4068 as you come to it on the outward route. Follow this 'B' road to the first crossroads in just over 1 mile and turn left to rejoin the return route above Upper Slaughter.

## Route

We start by the cafe and museum, next to the bridge over the stream, in Bourton-on-the-Water.

With your back to the stream cycle left down the main street; take this slowly and watch for coaches. You reach the A429 in a quarter of a mile, at which you turn right, with CARE, you may wish to walk across, and then left after a few yards. Turn right after 100 yards and continue for half a mile, climbing gently. Turn right at the junction, to reach Lower Slaughter in half a mile. The church and village proper lie ahead, and are well worth cycling round. To continue turn left, and with the stream to your left cycle on for half a mile, turning right at a small junction and then right again to enter Upper Slaughter. Once you have explored the village, leave by crossing the stream and cycling up a small hill for half a mile. Ignore a left turn and descend gently for half a mile to reach Lower Swell. Turn right at the B4068, with care, and after a few yards go ahead, as the 'B' road swings right.

Continue for just under 1 mile to the B4077. Upper Swell is to the right, but to continue turn left here and then, almost immediately, right, with care. After half a mile of pretty riding, the brewery appears to your left; 100 yards later, after a short climb, turn left round the brewery, riding parallel with the stream. Cycle on for 1 mile, ignoring a left turn but taking the first right. Turn left to cycle through Condicote, turning right round the church, and then bearing left after 300 yards. Turn left after 1 mile, to find woods on your right, and continue for under 1 mile, where you cross the B4077. Cycle on for 1.5 miles to arrive at a junction with a quarry ahead of you. Turn left and continue for two miles, including a climb, to reach an offset crossroads with Condicote Lane.

Turn right down the track, which is usually in good repair. One mile of Roman road later you reach the B4068. Go across here and then right after half a mile, to reach Upper Slaughter again in another half mile. Wiggle your way over the River Eye, pass the church, turn left and then right after 100 yards. Turn left in half a mile, after climbing the bank, and continue, mainly downhill, for 1 mile. At the A429 turn right, with CARE, and then left after 100 yards, to re-enter the main street of Bourton-on-the-Water. After a quarter of a mile will see you back at your starting point.

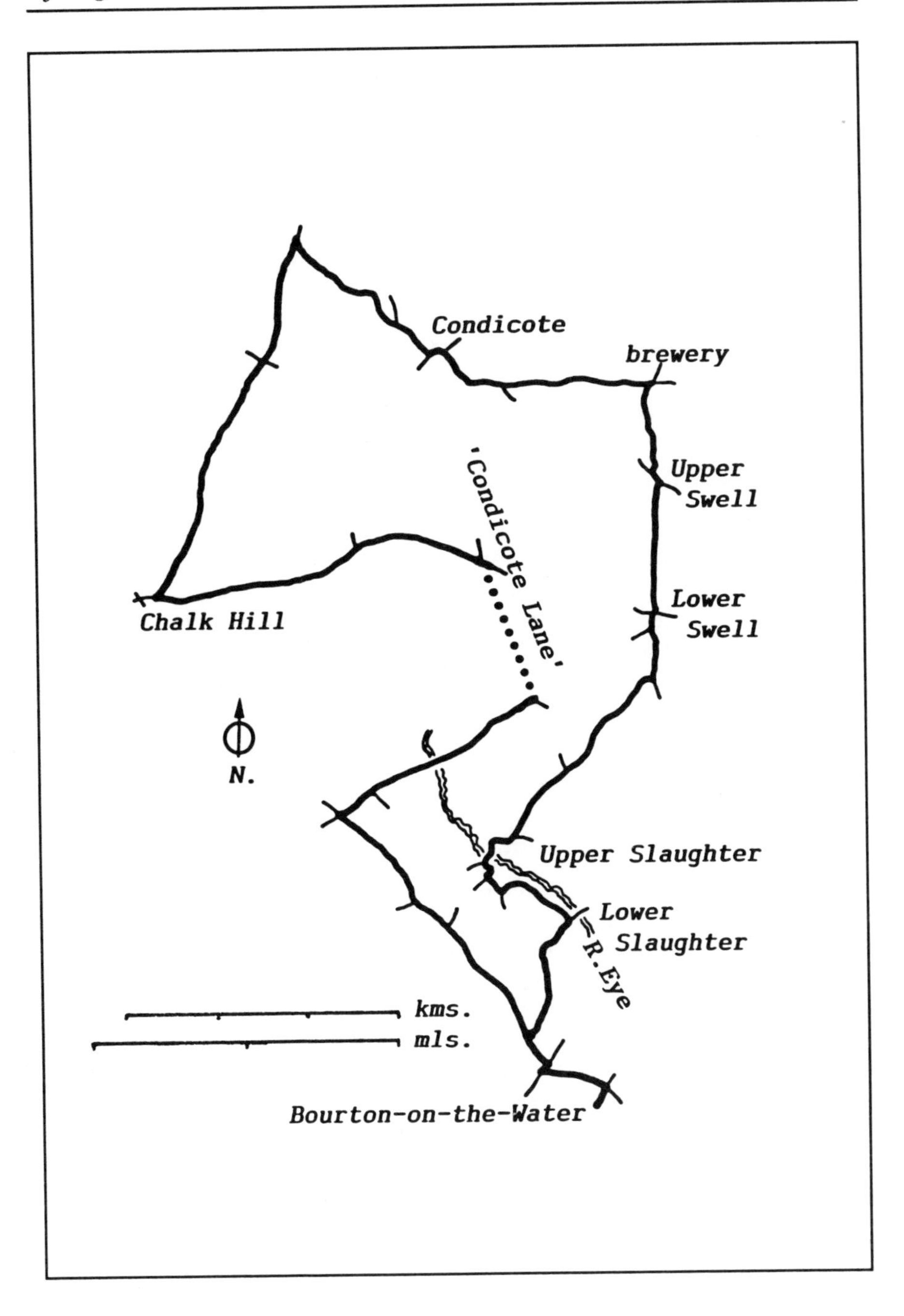
Condicote
brewery
Upper Swell
'Condicote Lane'
Lower Swell
Chalk Hill
N.
Upper Slaughter
Lower Slaughter
R.Eye
kms.
mls.
Bourton-on-the-Water

## Bourton-On-The-Water

Bourton-on-the-Water itself is best explored either in the morning before the coaches have arrived, or in the evening once they have left. Though it has some good features despite being swamped in the season, it is unique for a historical reason. While there are towns and villages in the area that date back centuries, 'lost' villages from before the Doomsday book, and ancient barrows, Bourton-on-the-Water is the only site in the Cotswolds that has been continually occupied since the Bronze age; that is to say for between 4,000 and 6,000 years. I wonder what the first inhabitants would make of the souvenir and fish and chip shops. (Probably eat the fish and chips and leave the souvenirs!)

## The Slaughters

You should simply enjoy the villages of Lower and Upper Slaughter. You pass through the villages twice, by different routes, and can weave back and forth along the lanes and over the tiny bridges which are perfect for cycling across. The name is nothing to do with killing and probably comes from the Anglo-Saxon for 'the place of the Sloes'. Before road maps and signposts natural objects, such as indigenous trees and shrubs, were useful waymarks. Other Cotswold examples are the yews at Uley, the hazels at Hazelton and the sapling pears at Sapperton.

Just to spoil things, however, another authority thinks that Slaughter comes from slough, meaning a muddy place, like the Slough of Despond, in the Pilgrim's Progress.

The top of the tower of Lower Slaughter church has recently been repaired. You can hardly see the join – though in these days of appearance than substance, the new piece is made from fibre glass!

## The Swells

Around the area to the west of the Swells are the remains of many long barrows. Some have never been excavated. Those that have prove to be from the Neolithic or Bronze Ages. The two at Pole's Wood, just to your left as you cycle between the Swells, held bones, including those of new born baby, a bronze razor, and evidence of large wooden buildings. The southern barrow had also been used much later as a Saxon burial site, and spearheads, brooches and beads were left with the bodies to accompany them to the afterlife.

Upper Swell is nicely clustered around the stream. The church of St.Mary has many features worth searching out, but I'll concentrate on only one. In many churches in this guide you will see font covers. Some

*Lower Slaughter*

are simple, some elaborate; the one at Northleach even has a sophisticated pulley system for raising and lowering the heavy wooden carving. In a wonderful example of the blend of superstition and Christianity, the reason for all these covers is to keep out witches. The witches were supposed to infect the water in the font with their evil powers, and thus taint the baby at Christening. The font at St.Mary's still has the staples intact for padlocking the cover in place. Perhaps the witches in Upper Swell were especially determined.

## Condicote

Condicote is an ancient place. A Roman road went through the village, or perhaps the village was built around the road; this Roman way was certainly built on the site of an even older tracks. The stone cross from the 1300s is still there in the centre of the village, which is surrounded by farm buildings. The church appears almost accidentally placed among the secular structures. Even if you don't have a mountain bike, do travel along Condicote Lane, either north or south, for a few yards to get a feel of this ancient route.

## The Brewery

The brewery at Donnington with its charming cluster of buildings, clear stream and near-by trout hatchery (we won't go into what fishes do in water) isn't open to visitors but it can be appreciated from the lanes on both sides. The water that feeds the lake, named the Dikler, is renamed Swell a little further along its course, to signify a stream of unpredictable course or intermittent appearance, but it looks well behaved here.

The stone for the brewery buildings is local, while the slates on the roofs are from Wales. The stream has been used for centuries. A mill was first established here in the 1300s, in the 1500s it became a cloth mill, and then a corn mill. The founder of the brewers, Thomas Arkell, bought the site in 1827, and by 1865 had changed the use from three mills, a bakehouse and a malthouse, to a brewery. Arkell's Donnington Ales are available later on the route.

# 12. 'A Sheep in a Church, and a Crocodile'

**Brief Description:** I have to be partial about this ride; it is one of my favourites. It has 2000 years of history, a chance of good food and drink, appearing at the right time on the route, quiet roads, hills high enough to give good views, but climbs not long enough to be dispiriting, and a village for a tea stop on your way 'home'. You'll discover the meaning of the cryptic title on your way around.

**Distance:** 25 miles/40 kms – The suggested short cut at Northleach will reduce this to 15 miles/24 kms.

**Terrain:** An up-and-down route, which will give you a full day's cycling, but no hill will take you longer than five minutes to climb, or a couple of minutes to descend.

When you see your descent is followed by another climb, find an appropriate gear, and before the hill starts to have an effect pedal like fury, using the speed you have built up. Change to a low gear ready to take up the pedalling once your momentum goes. In this way you should be half way up these short but sharp hills with hardly any effort. In some illustrations of this technique in older cycling books it is described as 'rushing the rise'.

**Rail Access:** Kingham is the nearest station to Bourton-on-the-Water, some 6 miles away.

**Links With:** The Slaughters and Kingham valley rides are also based on Bourton-on-the-Water. The Little Bit of Hell of the North Cotswolds ride passes through several villages on this route.

**Cutting It Short:** It would be a shame! But if you do wish to have a shorter or easier day the neatest short cut would be to find the A429 at Northlech. Turn right onto this road and then left after 250 yards to the village of Hampnett. Cycle through here to reach the A40 which you cross to join the return ride at Turkdean.

# Route

We start from the head of the town of Bourton-on-the-Water by the museum and cafe, and the green.

Cross the tiny bridge past the museum, up the lane past a coffee shop. The hill soon becomes quite fierce. Continue ahead at a junction after half a mile, and at another junction after a further mile. You'll know when you've reached the summit. Cycle on for 1.5 miles descending gently, before a short rise into Farmington. Bear right at the village green (though the church and dovecote are to your left here) and turn into a small left after 400 yards. Follow this lane for 1 mile, sneaking under the A40 on your way, before the quite fast descent into Northleach. You can go ahead at this point to continue but this avoids the centre of Northleach. A better alternative is to turn right, and then left around the market square, taking in the church on your way.

You leave Northleach by Mill End, passing the remains of a mill. After 1.5 miles of gentle progress, at a four-way junction go across/half right, and continue for 1 mile, to reach Coln St.Dennis. Turn right, passing the church to your left. Bear uphill, left and then ignore the sign for 'Fossebridge' designed for cars, and go ahead, with good hedges on either side. At the A429 do take CARE; you want to turn left for a few yards and then right across the main road. You may do best to cross on foot and then walk to the Fossebridge Inn.

Having perhaps made use of the pub, leave on foot up the hill, on the pub side of the road. Turn right after 50 yards. There are perfect views of farmland from this lane, which you follow for 1 mile, going ahead at the tiny cross roads. As the lane then turns hard right to Yanworth GO AHEAD into the lane of the Estate (you'll get to the villa even if you miss this junction). Continue along estate lane, which can be bumpy in places, with stream on your right. At the tarmac, after about 1 mile, turn left up a short hill to the villa.

Having seen the villa at Chedworth, return to this point and turn left, to follow the stream, which is again to your left. After half a mile of ancient meadowland you reach a large triangle of roads by excellent farm buildings. This is the ancient settlement of Casey Compton. Continue up to the buildings and turn right behind them. This small, rough section may force you to wheel your bike for a few yards by some good dry

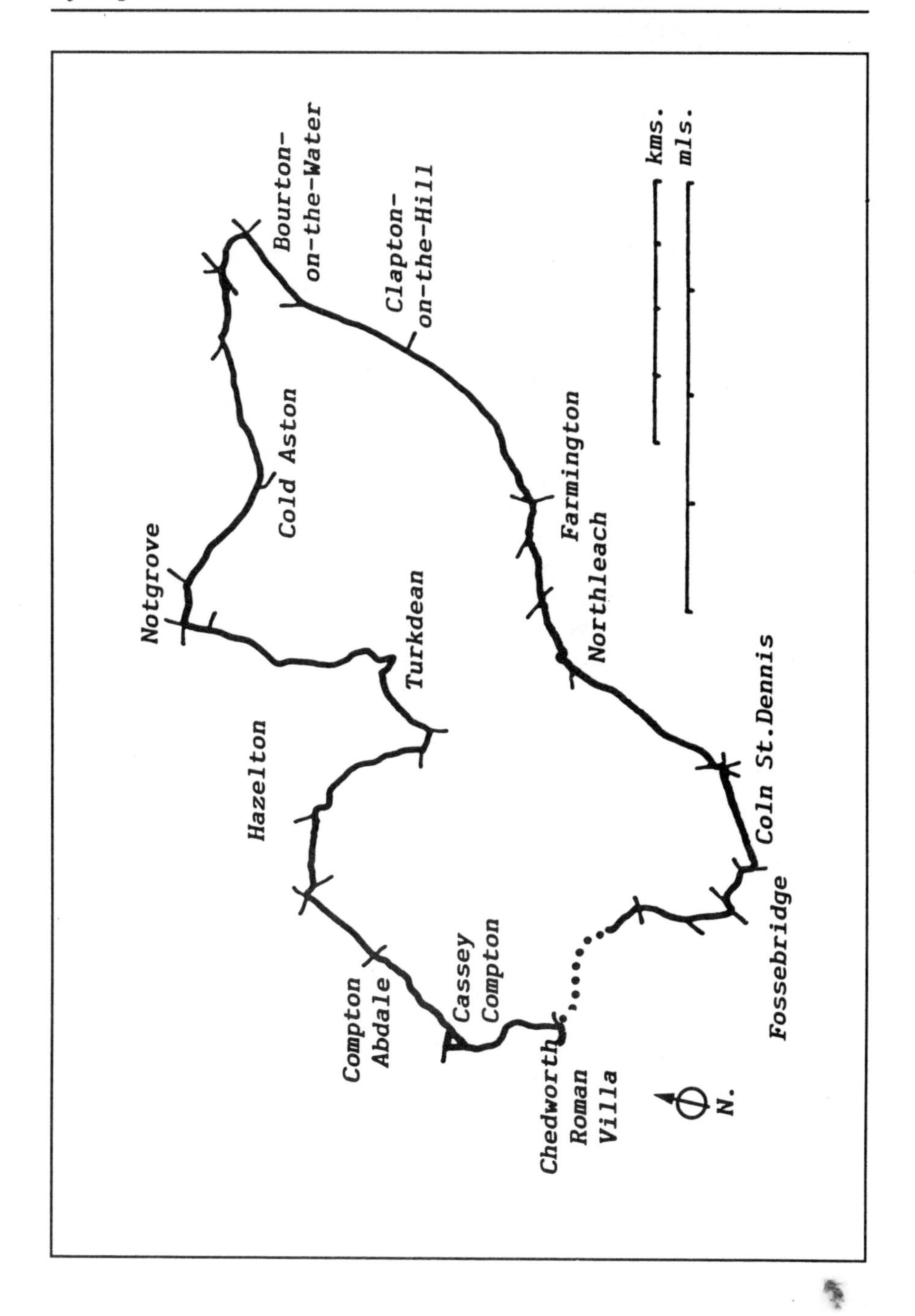
Bourton-
on-the-Water
Clapton-
on-the-Hill
kms.
mls.
Cold Aston
Farmington
Notgrove
Northleach
Turkdean
Coln St.Dennis
Hazelton
Fossebridge
Cassey
Compton
Compton
Abdale
Chedworth
Roman
Villa
N.

stone walling. At tarmac junction turn left up the short but sharp hill. Continue with woods on your right and views to your left for 1 mile, reaching Compton Abdale with a rush. At this crossroads the crocodile and church are to your left; the way out is ahead. If you don't wish to stop here, you should perhaps decide in advance and whizz through the village making best use of your momentum. Continue ahead out of the village climbing for a quarter of a mile to a fine summit with views. A quarter of a mile downhill follows to the BUSY A40. Go straight across with great care (perhaps on foot?), and then immediately right, onto a lane parallel with the main road. This turns away, and after half a mile you reach Hazleton.

Leave the village by the second right turn, though a circuit of the Hazleton takes you past the church and is only a few hundred yards. Continue for 1 mile, nearing the main road again, before taking two small left turns, which lead you, in 1 mile to a very sharp left and into Turkdean. Pass the church and leave the village ignoring two tracks. One and a half miles of happy riding will take you to Notgrove. Take the first right turn which leads you past the church. Continue through the village and then leave by turning right at the junction with only fields ahead. A mile further on, you reach Cold Aston, passing the church to your left, leaving by bearing left out of the village. A fine descent of 1 mile brings you to the A436, which you join, turning right and continuing downhill to the A429 at which you turn left. Turn first right WITH GREAT CARE after 200 yards to re-enter Bourton-on-the-Water by a lovely row of pollarded willow trees.

## Farmington

Farmington isn't on the tourist trail, despite being near Northleach and Bourton. I like this place, with its comfortable church, a grand house with a good dovecote which you can see from the lane, and a village green ideal for a few moments' rest. The small structure on the green was originally a pump-house, and was renovated in 1935 with the help of the residents of a Farmington, Connecticut, in America. On your way out of the village you'll see a perfectly built bus-shelter, made from local Cotswold stone. Just after the shelter, also on your right, you may notice the faint ramparts of Norbury camp, which the road slices in two. The supply of good stone may have helped the ancient people chose this site;

Farmington stone is still sought after, and the traces of stone mines are still found.

On your way from Farmington to Northleach, once you've passed under the 'A' road, don't cycle too fast or head down; the best views of the church and the village are before you reach it.

## Northleach

Northleach is rightly famous for its 'wool' church – that is, one built from the prosperity brought by wool. It is certainly worth exploring, and you should search for the sheep. The church is elaborate and has had money ostentatiously spent on it. The bizarre motivation of the benefactors seems clear; if you had the money you could try to buy your way to heaven. This doesn't take away from the beauty of the place, but helps to understand the large number of dedicated monuments and names everywhere.

Before we get carried away with the tranquil history and typical Cotswold beauty of Northleach, here is a passage that shows another side. Francis Witts was a diarist who travelled throughout the region and this is his entry for 12th. October 1827:

> *"I inspected the treadwheel at Northleach Bridewell, [prison] recently put up. The machinery still requires some alterations. The velocity with which the wheel revolved was too great, so that the fatigue exceeded the strength of the prisoners. The revolutions should be limited to about 52 steps in a minute. A regulator must be applied to the machine in such a manner as to compensate for any difference in the weight of the gangs on the wheel, whether grown men or boys.*
>
> *The millwright was in attendance. It is intended to keep the machine going, should there be at any time be a failure of corn to grind. Nine or ten prisoners were on the mill at once, they worked each $4^1/_2$ or 5 minutes, one descending from the proximity of the wheel every half minute. A relay of prisoners is kept in an adjacent yard, walking in a circle".*

These 'grown men or boys' could be on this treadmill for stealing a cabbage, or a loaf of bread.

## Coln St.Dennis

I do like the unassuming church of St. James at Coln St. Dennis. Why it's not dedicated to St. Dennis I don't know. There are flowers at the front of the churchyard, while the interior is calm and human sized. The lovely solid door dates from 1637. Walk around the outside before you cycle on, and you'll see the rather drunken looking south wall, which looks as though it will fall at any moment.

## Chedworth Roman Villa

The villa in the woods at Chedworth is perfectly approached by bicycle, as you catch the first view of the substantial remains through the trees. Except for the incongruous building in the centre of the site, which now houses the museum, the view is little different from the one the Romans would have had. For details of what to you can see consult a guide, written or human, at the site. The spring, at the corner of the villa has an unusual dedication and probably had mystical or religious significance well (!) before the Romans arrived. Certainly it was taken over by the Saxons once the Romans had left.

Opening times vary at different times of the year; it is closed on Mondays. Details from 0242 89256.

## Compton Abdale

The Crocodile is the name given to the elongated water duct that directs the stream just below the church at Compton Abdale. Souvenir mugs with this unusual decoration are available from the church, which is also worth inspecting for its ghastly gargoyles and corbel stones. What are those animals standing on each corner of the tower? Bears?

## A Trio of Villages

Each of the villages of Hazleton, Turkdean, Notgrove and Cold Aston has a different character. All are quiet; this is an especially peaceful part of the Cotswolds, despite being close to Bourton-under-the-Tourist. All are tightly grouped together around the church or largest house. There is little water in this higher area, and by living closely together the practicalities of sharing out the limited supply were eased.

*Compton Abdale*

## Hazleton

St.Andrews church at Hazleton has some interesting tombs in the graveyard. The Cistercian monks from Kingswood, near Wotton-under-Edge, tried to settle here to escape the chaos and violence of King Stephen's rule from 1135 to 1154, but were defeated by the lack of water, mentioned above.

## Turkdean

Turkdean still has fine beechwoods; the beech has been called the 'weed of the Wolds'. It has three manor houses, each built by succeeding authorities over this tiny village. In the 1820's, when food was very scarce, this was the site of the 'Battle of Turkdean', between gamekeepers and four poachers. A gamekeeper was killed and the poachers were put on trial. To most people's surprise they were acquitted by a sympathetic jury. Even the judge thought that the poachers had 'a most extraordinary escape'.

## Notgrove

The church at Notgrove was built on the site of a Saxon one, and close to a Roman graveyard. The font shows its Norman origins. If you have time to cycle round the village you will get a good feel for the way that the settlement has grown, while still remaining in a close cluster round the church.

## Cold Aston

Several estates around here were enclosed in the early 1800s to maximise the income for the landowners. At Cold Aston a mason from Turkdean, John Wright, was employed to build the stone walls around the vicar's allotment, in lieu of tithes. The contract insisted that they were to be no less than four feet and eight inches high, and came with a repairing clause to last for seven years. For this work John Wright was allowed £10 per furlong (220 yards) off his dues. Whether you can still see his work in Cold Aston, I'm not sure, but there are excellent examples of Cotswold dry stone walling around the village. It is 'dry' because it is made without 'wet' cement or mortar.

# 13. 'A Little Bit of Hell of The North Cotswolds'

**Brief Description:** This very strange name for a supposedly pleasurable cycle ride has an interesting history. Every year in early April the classic Paris Roubaix cycle race takes place, much it over the *'pavé'* (cobblestones). The road surface, together with the time of year, combine to give a very hard ride. It is known as *'L'Enfer du Nord'*, 'The Hell of the North'. In 1987 the Winchcombe Cycling Club decided to create a homegrown version of the ride and designed a route to give as much track and by-way cycling as possible. Their route is a reliability trial during which 50 miles has to be covered in six hours. Our version is shorter, more gentle, and avoids most of the steeper climbs but still takes you off the tarmac road. Condicote Lane is a portion of Roman road which still feels like one; half close the eyes and listen for the sound of the legions on the march. Even if you walk some sections I'd recommend this route as a way of seeing sights that most won't! Fords are included and they are always fun on a bicycle. If you are in a group, send one of the party ahead with the camera to wait by the ford; the quality of the shots is then up to you!

**Distance:** 31 miles/50 kms.

**Terrain:** Some of the tracks can be rough, others are more like 'normal' roads. Heavy rain followed by use of the bridleways by horses can make the surface sticky and muddy, though they are well drained in the higher areas of the wolds. In drier weather you should be happy to cycle the bridleways. If you feel unsteady in some sections just dismount and push your cycle for a while. This is not 'cheating'; you're meant to be enjoying yourself. There are some climbs out of the valleys, but maintain a steady pace and you'll make good progress.

**Rail Access:** The nearest station is Kingham, 6 miles from Bourton-on-the-Water. At Condicote you are slightly closer to Moreton-in-Marsh Station on the same line.

Links With: The Slaughters, Kingham valley and Chedworth rides are also based on Bourton-on-the-Water. You pass through several of the same villages as the Chedworth ride, though by different routes. You are within half a mile of Stanway as you gain the B4077 at the north-western corner of the ride. Stanway is on the Sudeley Castle route, based on Winchcombe.

**Cutting It Short:** There are so many opportunities to miss out sections of this route, that details are not given. Some short cuts will simply shorten the mileage, while others will avoid bridle-paths, using tarmac instead.

# Route

We start this ride from Bourton-on-the-Water, by the cafe and museum at the head of the stream, by the bridge. If you are forced to transport your cycles by car then you can start at almost anywhere on the route, but do park sensitively: avoid blocking gates and farm entrances.

This route could also be joined from Winchcombe, but this would start with the climb up Sudeley Hill.

Leave Bourton-on-the-Water by turning left along the main street. At the A429 which you reach in a quarter of a mile, turn right, with care and then first left after 100 yards. Continue for 1 mile before turning right to Upper Slaughter. Cycle through the village, crossing the stream, and leave by the lane uphill ahead of you. In just over half a mile, take the first left. You are now on Ryknild Street. You follow this road ahead, across all junctions, for over three miles, until you arrive at Condicote. In detail this is as follows: ahead for half a mile to the B4068; across the 'B' road; ahead for under 1 mile to go straight across an offset junction; continue for 1 mile to reach the B4077; ahead at this offset junction and in half a mile you will reach Condicote.

Bear left twice at Condicote, and then turn left 150 yards outside the village. Turn first left after 1 mile and then first right in another mile, onto the B4077. Continue on the 'B' road for 1.5 miles, when you turn right at the first crossroads. Cycle on (very) straight ahead for 1.5 miles, ignoring the first left at 1 mile, to a crossroads. Turn left down the lane at this junction. Continue for 1 mile to go straight across at the first junction. In 500 yards again go ahead along the track through Lidcombe Wood. In over half a mile you reach tarmac at the B4077 where you turn left. Continue for 1 mile. At the first junction, where a road comes in from your left, turn right, down a track. Continue for 1.25 miles to reach tarmac again, at the junction of two roads.

Go ahead here, not hard right, turning first left in half a mile. Bear left after a quarter of a mile, and left again after another quarter of a mile. In half a mile you cycle through a wood, and emerge from it after 100 yards. Just as you clear the wood, having it only on your left, you will see two bridle-paths ahead, going right. Take the left-hand path. In a quarter of a mile the track joins a surfaced path which then passes Roel Hill farm, to reach tarmac in another half a mile. At the road turn right

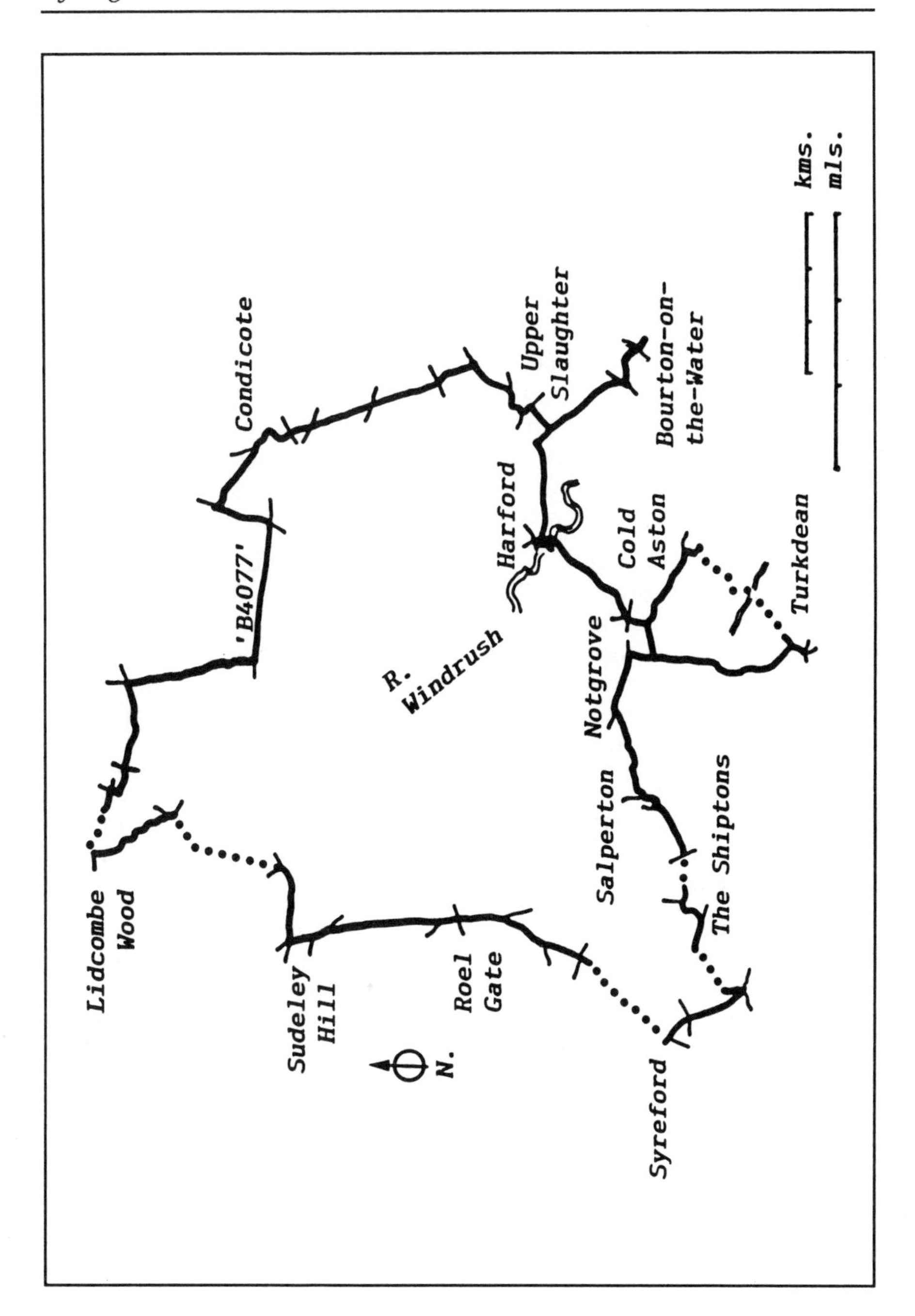
Condicote
Upper Slaughter
Bourton-on-the-Water
kms.
mls.
'B4077'
Harford
Cold Aston
Turkdean
R. Windrush
Notgrove
Salperton
The Shiptons
Lidcombe Wood
Sudeley Hill
Roel Gate
Syreford
N.

for a quarter of a mile. At the crossroads turn left and continue for just over half a mile. Bear right at the fork, ignore a right turn after half a mile, and continue for another half a mile to a 'T' junction. The tarmac goes to left and right, your route lies along the track straight ahead, starting to the right of the building. Continue for 1.25 miles, to reach tarmac again. Turn left, passing over the disused railway, to the A436. Cross the 'A' road, with care, and continue, reaching Shipton in one mile.

Take the first left in the village, cycle on to the end of the row of cottages, and follow the track that continues between the last two buildings. In just over half a mile you reach tarmac again. Turn right, and then first left in a quarter of a mile, to reach the hamlet of Hampen in a few hundred yards. Turn right by the last building, and before the remains of the railway, along a track for half a mile. Go ahead at the crossroads on tarmac again, reaching Salperton in half a mile.

Turn right at the rounded 'T' junction in Salperton, and then right again after 150 yards, to leave the village down a tiny lane. This track plays with the dismantled railway, going over and through it before surprisingly reaching the A436 after 1 mile. Turn right with CARE, onto the 'A' road, which comes as a shock after so much quiet riding, and continue for half a mile, before taking the first right, with care. A quarter of a mile later you reach Notgrove.

If you wish to miss out the loop from Notgrove, passing through Turkdean and Cold Aston, via Bang-Up Barn, take the first left in the village, and first left again after a quarter of a mile to reach the A436. Pick up directions by simply skipping the next paragraph.

To continue on the Notgrove loop go ahead, ignoring a second left turn into the village, and continue for 1.25 miles to reach the edge of Turkdean. To explore the village and church, go ahead a few yards, but to continue turn left between two farm buildings. This is the route of an ancient track. Continue for almost 2 miles, first descending to a stream and then rising again to pass Bangup Barn, and entering Cold Aston 400 yards later. At Cold Aston, turn left, though the church and pub are a few yards to your right, and continue for one straight mile to a junction at which you turn half right. 300 yards later you reach the A436.

At the A436 go straight across, with care, into the lane and then immediately right. In just over 1 mile you reach the settlement of

Harford. Go through the ford at least once; it's a good chance to wash your wheels and maybe yourself! Bear left up to the 'B' road and turn right, and immediately right again along another lane (not along the 'B' road). In 1 mile turn right, and after another mile you should recognise where you are: back at the A429. Turn right with care, and first left after

*Condicote Lane*

a few yards to re-enter Bourton-on-the-Water. The town centre lies half a mile ahead.

There are fewer descriptions of attractions on this ride. Not because there is nothing to see but the very point of this route is that it takes you off the normal ways. Several villages that you pass by, or through, are covered in two other rides based on Bourton-on-the-Water.

There are few descriptions of the villages, and other attractions you pass through on this ride; some are covered in more detail on the Chedworth route. This is not because there is nothing to see but the very nature of this route is that it takes you away from larger settlements.

Concentrate instead on the rabbits that scuttle away as you approach, the spring flowers, including bluebells that glow in the wooded sections or the flocks of birds that you put up. I have been lucky enough to see the hazy blue flash of a hobby, a bird of prey, on this ride.

# 14. 'The White Way'

**Brief Description:** The White Way is the name given to a small but important Roman Road linking Cirencester, which the Romans called *Corinium Dobunnorum*, with the villas and other settlements to the north. These included Spoonley, Wadfield, and Chedworth which is featured on another route in this book. The church at North Cerney, with its paintings, gargoyles and medieval stained glass, is a 'must', despite its proximity to the rather noisy main road. Each of the Duntisbournes – Abbots, Leer and Rous – has a distinct feel and its own reason to make you stop and look. The fords are all worth several splashes through.

**Distance:** 20 miles/32 kms.

**Terrain:** There is an initial rise up onto the White Way, but the Romans didn't like sharp climbs any more than cyclists do. At the northern section of the route, before turning south toward Elkstone you have gained a good amount of height which you loose only gradually. Apart from dropping in to the Duntisbournes themselves the return to Cirencester is fine ridge riding.

**Rail Access:** The nearest station to Cirencester is Kemble, on the Swindon – Cheltenham line. This is about 3 miles away on either the A429 or the quieter route via Ewen and Siddington.

**Links With:** The other route from Cirencester is along Akeman Street to the east. At the point at which you turn left off the White Way to North Cerney, if you continue along the Roman road you reach Cassey Compton on the Chedworth ride in just four miles.

**Cutting It Short:** You can miss the northern part of the ride by continuing west, ahead, after North Cerney. This will bring you to the return route, via Bagendon, at Middle Duntisbourne.

# Route

We start from outside the Tourist Information Centre in Cirencester.

With your back to the Tourist office, cycle off left, passing the church on your right. Go ahead into Castle Street at the first junction. At the end of Castle Street in 100 yards, turn right into Park Lane. This then becomes Park Street and then Thomas Street. At the offset and busy junction with Dollar Street go across into Spitalgate. After 300 yards, at the junction with the A417, which is controlled by traffic lights, go straight across. You are now on the White Way; even the road signs say so! Continue for 3 miles, climbing gently at some points, going ahead at the two crossroads at 2 and 2.5 miles. Turn left at the third crossroads, without buildings by it, and after half a mile a quick descent leads you into North Cerney. By the usually pink pub, cross the A435 (CARE: perhaps on foot?) to reach the church.

After exploring the church at North Cerney, leave by the road at the rear of the churchyard, around Cerney House. At the small crossroads after 400 yards turn right, and continue ahead for 1 mile to reach Woodmancote. Bear right in the village, and then left on leaving it. Turn right after 1 mile, with a wood in front of you, left after 400 yards, and continue with pylons to your right for 1 mile. At the intricate junction go across/half left. Continue for a gently undulating 1 mile with excellent views, to reach a crossroads. Turn left here, signed to Elkstone and cycle on for half a mile to reach Elkstone Church. Having visited the church, continue, up and down a dip after the village, to regain the ridge.

In 1 mile at the junction with A417, by the Highwayman pub, go straight across, and you reach Winstone in half a mile. Turn right and right through the village (the church however is first left), and just out of the village go left, ignoring the tiny right by Gaskill's Farm. If you like rough riding and have a suitable bike you can bear left after a 100 yards or so down the 'Unsuitable for Motors' track to Duntisbourne Abbotts. Otherwise continue for 1 mile, over the summit of the route, before taking the second left turn at Jackbarrow Farm. Freewheel into the valley and after half a mile you will arrive at Duntisbourne Abbots.

At the first junction you can turn right and onto the other Duntisbourne, but this misses the church and ford. Cycle to the church, swing right and then right again downhill through the village and the splash. Turn right at a small 'T' junction at 400 yards, and left after a few yards. Continue for 2 miles, passing through Duntisbourne Leer and Middle Duntisbourne, and by Duntisbourne Rouse on your way, to reach Daglingworth.

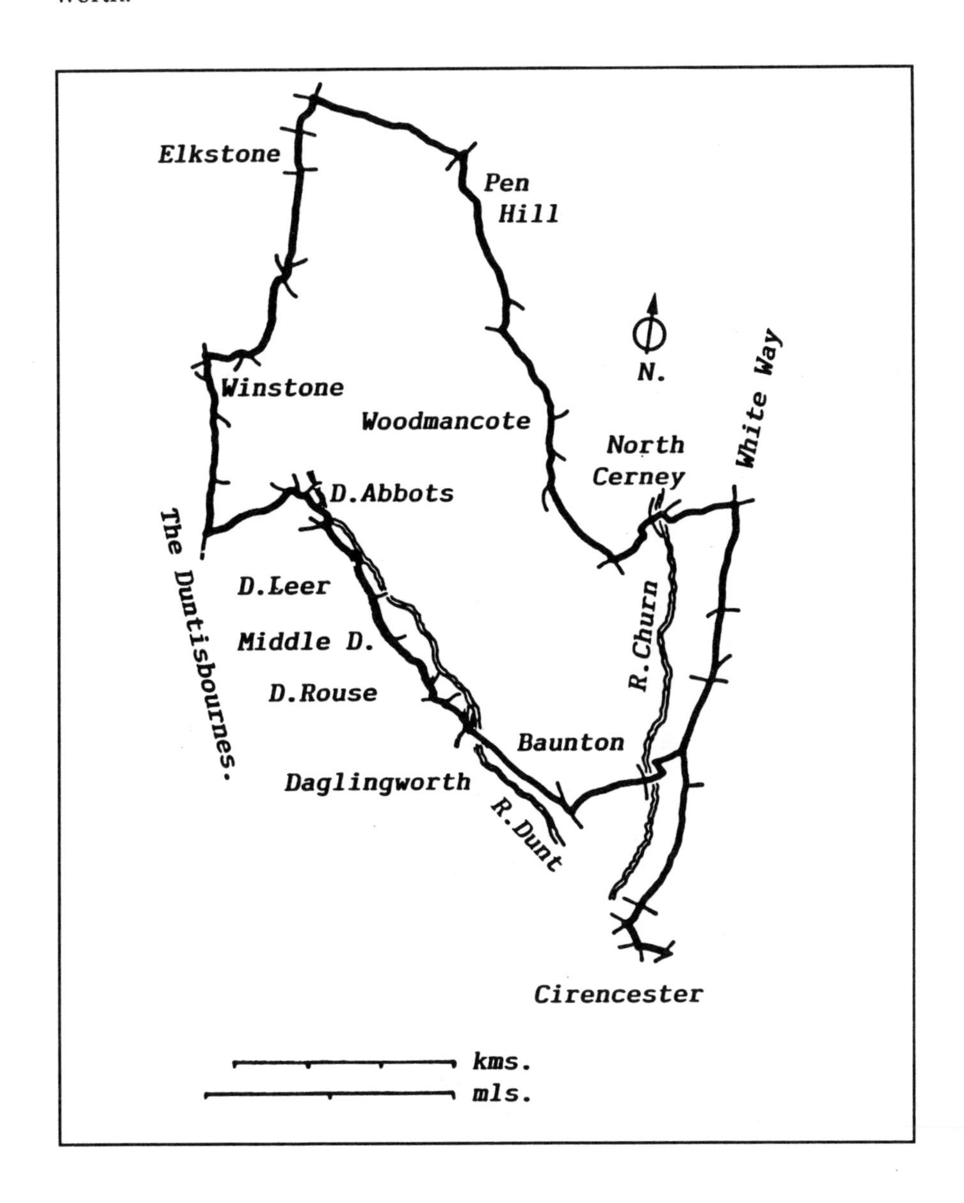

As you reach the village the Dunt to your left appears to flow through the field with almost nothing to contain it. At the 'T' in the village turn left and then follow bends through village for a quarter of a mile, with the church on your right. After one mile you meet the A417 with a church to your right. Here you turn right and then left after a few yards into Baunton Lane (you may prefer to cross this busy road on foot). In half a mile there is another crossing of an 'A' road, this time straight across. 400 yards on, having crossed the stream, you meet your outward route again, turning right, and after 1 mile of pleasant downhill, and good views of the town ahead, you re-enter Cirencester.

## White Way

The two miles of Romanly straight road before you turn off the ridge to North Cerney, form a lovely and unspoilt section of the White Way. You can imagine the regular trips for trade, business or even pleasure from Cirencester to the villa at Chedworth. It seems that this part of the track was in regular use before the Romans came, demonstrating one of their successful traits: adopt and adapt.

## North Cerney

North Cerney church, across the A435 from the Bathurst Arms Pub, has been restored, but sensitively. It is the third building on the site. Don't miss the wall painting of the manticore, a half lion, half man. There is stained glass from the 1400s and a Norman altar, only re-discovered in 1912, which weighs a ton and a half. I particularly like the four heads on the lintel over the north door. Do allow some time to look round All Saints.

## Elkstone

The Doomsday book describes Elkstone, from the Saxon, as The Stone of Ealac. A stone in the excellent Norman church of St.John is thought to be the one after which the village is named. Who Ealac was we don't know. If you look for the stone in the church do also notice the gargoyles; some seem to be playing music, while another is a serpent biting its' own body. You can tell why the doorway is famous. The tympanum is surrounded by the beakhead arch, with human heads inset. What are all those other heads? The central one looks to me like a cuttlefish. The slightly squashed figure above the arch could almost be a grinning cat. Further inside, the window behind the altar, usually the largest and most grand, is tiny. Look up as you stand in front of the altar to see the carved belt and buckle, seemingly holding the roof arches together.

## Duntisborne Leer

Duntisborne Leer ford was created to provide a bath for washing tools and horses after a muddy day in the fields. This also had the advantage of swelling, and therefore tightening, the joints of the wooden wheels. The village is called Leer as it originally belonged to the Abbey of Lire in northern France, showing the extent of monastic influence before the dissolution.

## Duntisbourne Rous

While Leer and Middle have lost their churches, Duntisbourne Rous church has lost its village, and now stands almost alone. It is built on a bank and this gave enough space to construct a crypt even in this tiny building.

*Lych Gate to St Michael at Duntisbourne Rous*

## Daglingworth

Holy Rood church at Daglingworth has many restored Saxon carvings, some reset, others where they have been since it was built. When the Normans rebuilt part of the church they remove some Saxon carvings but replaced the stones with the decoration pointing inwards. So when the church was later restored in 1845-50, these carvings were seen for the first time for perhaps 800 years. I like the Saxon sundial above the south door. How many sunrises and sunsets has it recorded since it was put in place? From the same period and also at the south door you can see some tiny carvings of ears of wheat, a clear blend of ancient fertility beliefs and the 'new' Christian church.

One of the Saxon carvings shows Christ with two other figures, one of whom is holding the sponge soaked in vinegar. This action by the Roman soldier is usually taught as a further example of the mocking Christ on the cross. This shows a lack of understanding of one of the Romans' habits: vinegar, often diluted with water, was a common drink among Romans, especially on the march. It was refreshing and helped to purify the water, which was often brackish. So the offer of a sponge full of vinegar was an act of kindness.

Daglingworth House, next to the church, has by it a dovecote with space for over 500 birds and a revolving ladder for inspecting them. Doves and their less decorative relative, the pigeon, were first kept as a source of meat. It was only later that the better-off could afford to keep them almost as pets. This must have caused envy and anger among their hungry neighbours.

## Baunton

As you swing east through Baunton and cross the Churn you should spot some ditches and mounds on the banks of the river. These are the remains of a network of sluice gates. These were not used to water the crops, but on cold winter nights the gates were opened to flood the meadows. This protected the crops from frost; the water was drained away again in the morning. Before specialist early seed varieties were available this must have been a great advance, both for fodder and produce. This practice only ceased just before the First World War.

Given the above, it is perhaps appropriate that the wall painting in Baunton church features St.Christopher wading through a stream filled with brown and green fish. Dating from the 1300s, the paintings also show a farming scene, complete with a windmill.

## Cirencester

William Cobbett in his 'Rural Rides' is as scathing as usual about Cirencester, or rather the effect the Corn Laws and other political mismanagement had upon the people. To him, even the 'negroes' in America, where he had lived for twenty years, had a better life.

*"The labourers seem miserably poor. Their dwellings are little better than pig-beds, and their looks indicate that their food is not nearly equal to that of a pig. Their wretched hovels are struck upon little bits of ground on the road side . . . it seems as if they had been swept off the fields by a hurricane, and had dropped and found shelter under the banks on the road side!*

*And this is 'Prosperity' is it? These O Pitt! are the fruits of your hellish system!...This is the country that the Gallon loaf man belongs to. The land all along here is good. Fine fields and pastures all around; and yet the cultivators of those fields so miserable!"*

Pitt of course was the Tory Prime Minister at the time. Cobbett thought that he could organise society in a far better way and his 'Cottage Economy' became a handbook for the 'two acres and a cow' way of living.

# 15. 'Akeman Street'

**Brief Description:** Half of this ride takes a happily meandering course from Cirencester, while the return is, for much of its route, on a direct and straight Roman Road. Akeman Street used to run all the way from Cirencester, through Bicester, to St.Albans. For some of its length it has been taken over by cars and their main roads, while elsewhere it is only a line on a map. Happily there are some stretches where the Romans' gift for picking a good line for a road is still of use to cyclists. They wanted good visibility, to watch for malevolent Britons of various tribes, and as direct a route as possible without too steep a gradient. The hedges and general feel of Quenington, and the twin churches and clapper bridge at Eastleach are two particular features that you'll enjoy. Leaving Cirencester by the south makes a quieter and safer beginning; the return to Corinium Dobrinium largely by the Roman road seems appropriate.

**Distance:** 38 miles/61 kms – The suggested short cut reduces this to 21 miles/34 kms.

**Terrain:** With large expanses of water around the start of this route is flat as you'd expect. Toward the eastern point of the route there are some wriggles into, and then out of, small valley bottoms. None of these is a serious climb. Most of the return, largely along the course of Roman Akeman Street, is a level ride along the ridge, but with enough undulations to keep the view changing.

**Rail Access:** The nearest station to Cirencester is Kemble, unofficially called 'Cirencester Parkway' by some railway staff, about 3.5 miles away. You can cycle from Kemble on the A429, or the more pleasant but slightly less direct route via Ewen and Upper Siddington, picking up the route at the village.

**Links With:** The White Way route to the north is also based on Cirencester. The ride to the east of Malmesbury passes through Kemble and Coates. At Holwell, the extreme east of this ride, you are within 2 miles of Burford (ahead to Westwell and then right), which in turn links with two other rides.

**Cutting It Short:** The neatest way of shrinking this ride is to cycle north at Down Ampney to reach Meysey Hampton, crossing the A417, before joining the return route, on Akeman Street, at Ready Token.

## Route

We start this ride at the Tourist Information Centre in Cirencester.

With your back to the Tourist centre, turn left to follow the main street round with the church to your right. Go ahead at the junction into Castle Street. At the end of Castle Street turn left into Sheep Street, bearing left at a mini-roundabout to continue in Sheep Street and then bearing right into Querns Hill to cross the dual-carriageway. Once over the bridge bear left into Somerford Road and into Somerford Road again at a cross roads with Chesterton Lane after 300 yards. Cycle on for 1 mile, ignoring the first left turn, bearing right but taking the second left to Siddington. You pass through Lower Siddington, and reach the main village after half a mile. Continue, crossing the River Churn and immediately turn right. Cycle on for 2 miles down the Churn valley, the river is to your right, to reach South Cerney.

Enter the village of South Cerney, with the lane to the church on your left, and at a 'T' junction turn left. Continue for 1 mile, with water to left and right, to the B4696. Cross straight over and wind your way through the water park, reaching Cerney Wick in 1 mile. In the village turn left, before the 'phone box, to cross the course of the disused canal by a pub, arriving at the A419 in half a mile.

Cross the 'A' road, with great CARE, to head for Down Ampney, which you reach in 1 mile. To visit the church you take the first small right in the village; to continue take the second small right, 400 yards later. Continue for a flat 1.5 miles to reach a 'T' junction at which you turn left. Cycle ahead for 1.5 miles to enter Kempsford. The church by the river is down the lane to your right; to continue you must turn left, to cycle on for 1.5 miles, with the edge of the airfield on your left. When you reach Whelford continue ahead through the village, crossing the River Coln and with views of water ahead of you. (If you wish to visit Fairford turn left in Whelford, reaching Fairford in 1 mile).

Cycle on through the water park for 1 mile to reach the A417. Here you turn left and then almost immediately right. This small lane crosses the sadly disused railway, and then at a 'T' junction in a quarter of a mile turn right. Cycle on for two straight miles, through two tiny crossroads, to reach a 'T' junction. Turn right here to visit Southrop: church, manor, pub, river. To continue turn left, reaching Eastleach Turville in 1 mile.

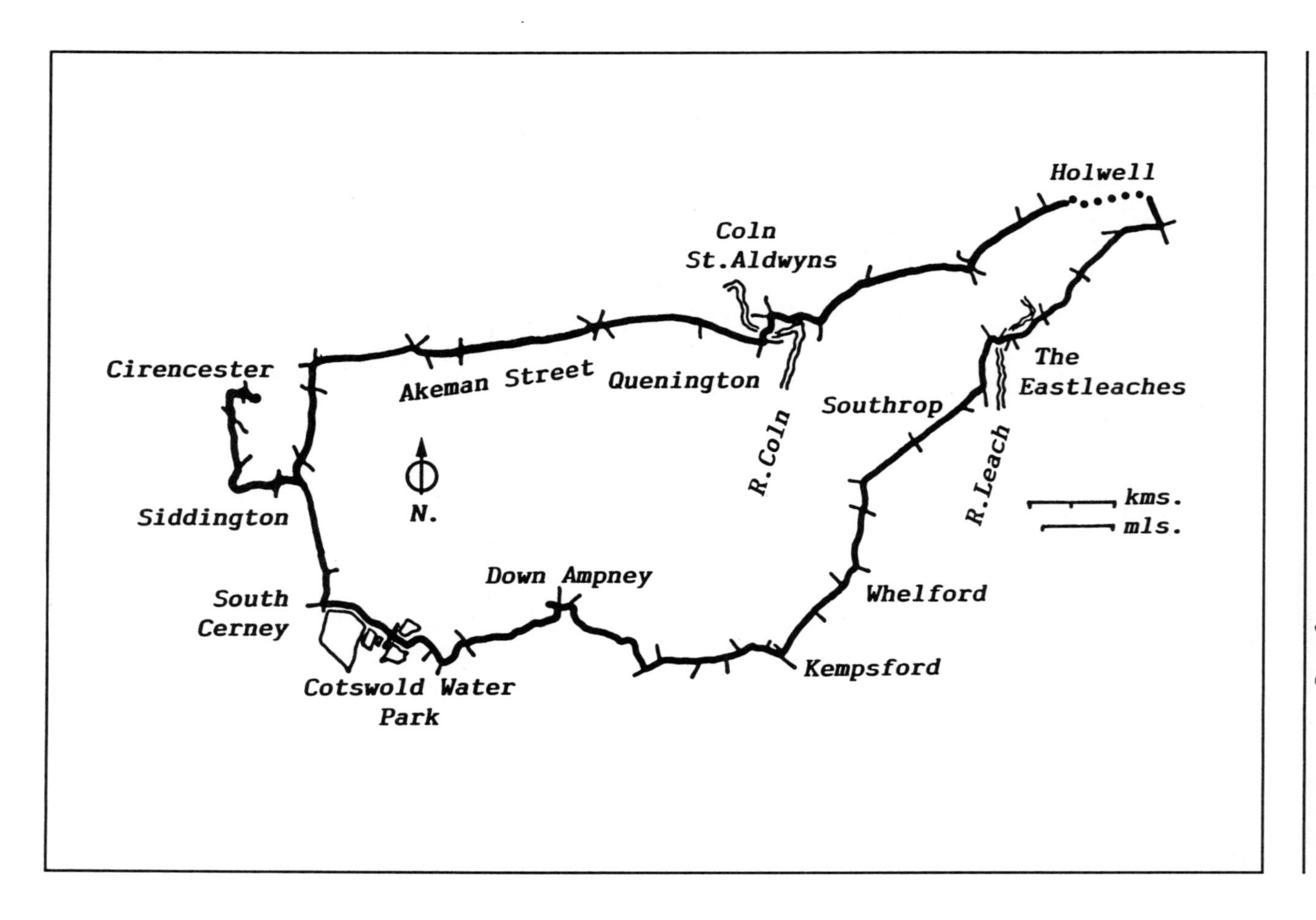
Holwell
Coln St.Aldwyns
Cirencester
Akeman Street
Quenington
The Eastleaches
Southrop
R.Coln
R.Leach
kms.
mls.
N.
Siddington
Down Ampney
Whelford
South Cerney
Kempsford
Cotswold Water Park

Wind your way through the village, perhaps cycling around it and its near neighbour of Eastleach Martin, several times. To continue head between the two churches, and over a bridge, to a small crossroads and turn left to follow the stream, which will be on your left. Go across at a crossroads after half a mile and again after another half mile, turning right at an offset junction in another half mile. You are now on your first stretch of Akeman Street. Continue to a crossroads at half a mile, and turn left here, to reach Holwell in half a mile.

Turn left in the village of Holwell, before the chapel, (not half left), down a bridle-path/farm track to Holwell Downs Farm. The surface is rough in places but the way is flat. Pass through the farm after 1 mile, reaching a junction in a further 300 yards. Turn left here, and continue ahead for 1.5 miles to a junction in a dip by a stream. Take the second right, having crossed the stream. Continue ahead for 2 miles, initially along the very straight Akeman Street, before swinging left to reach Hatherop. Take the first right in the village, passing first the church and then the stream to your left, to reach Coln St.Aldwyns in half a mile. Turn left at a slightly offset 'T' junction with the church ahead of you, to pass a pub and then cycle next to the River Coln for 400 yards, before crossing it to reach Quenington. The village and its many attractions lies ahead; to continue cycle on to the second crossroads at which you should turn right. Turn right again after half a mile by a farm, and after another half mile, with woods either side, turn left at a 'T' junction. You regain the course of Akeman Street in a few hundred yards. Go ahead at a crossroads in half a mile, and then bear left after a few yards to continue on the Roman road. Cycle (very) straight on for 2 miles until you reach the B4425. Turn left here and after 1.25 miles at the A429, turn left again.

[You can go ahead here to Cirencester on the 'A' road but it is busy, fast and forces you to use a roundabout on a dual carriageway. The recommended route therefore skirts the town].

Having turned left at the 'A' road, continue for a quarter of a mile, go straight across the A417, with care, and 1 straight mile later cross the A419 with even more care, perhaps on foot. In a quarter of a mile turn right to re-enter Siddington. You now follow your outward route in reverse, namely: left and then first right in the village, continue half a mile and then turn right at a 'T' junction. Continue for 1 mile, bearing left after half a mile, to re-enter Cirencester.

## South Cerney

If you stop to look at the doorway of the church at South Cerney you'll be able to compare the sculpture with that at Quenington later on the ride. Some authorities think it was carved by the same people or the same firm, but being 'authorities' they call it the same school.

## Down Ampney

John Leland mentions a journey through the Ampneys in his 'Itenerary', written in the mid-1500s. He spells them 'Amney', and the locals today still ignore the 'p'. The Isis is the Thames.

> *"Ther cummith a litle bek by Pulton, that after goit at a mille a litle aboe Dounamney village into Amney water, into the Isis".*

> *"Amney brook risith a litle above Amney toune by north out of a rok: and goith a 3 miles of or moe to Dounamney wher Syr Antony Hungreford hath a fair house of stone".*

The 'fair house of stone' is still there, though it has suffered from two fires over the intervening years. The front of Down Ampney House bears several shields of the Hungerford family, and a memorial to the same Sir Antony Hungerford is in the pretty village church by the house. Ralph Vaughan-Williams, one of the most 'English' of English composers, was born in the village in 1872. He wrote the best known tune to the hymn 'The day thou gavest Lord, has ended', which is called 'Down Ampney'.

You'll need to take a diversion of a few hundred yards to see the church and house.

## Kempsford

Kempsford church is on a mound, close to the Thames. This was the site of a Saxon ford across the river. I suppose it was later that the crossing point was named after Mr. or Mrs. or Ms. Kemp. The church itself is looked after exceptionally well, and has a set of four pennant weather-vanes on its tower. It is one of the most intact Norman buildings in the Cotswolds. The nave has its four original windows built in about 1120. There are special views to the west and south, where the disuse of the ford has prevented building by the bank of the river.

## Southrop

Our route just misses Southrop village. But if you appreciate the varied Norman work of the Cotswolds you'll want to take the small diversion to St.Peters church. The font is one of the best. There are carvings of virtues, shown as women with armour, conquering the vices, whose names are spelt backwards, presumably so that they would be less impressive. Others show Moses and the tables of the law.

## The Eastleaches

The clapper bridge at Eastleach Martin is known as Keble's Bridge, after the family of that name who owned the nearby estate. Once *in situ* these structures obviously last well; building them without modern lifting machinery must have required many people's effort, and well organised too. The far more ancient stone bridge at Chagford in Devon is a very similar simple design. While off your bike looking at the bridge, spend a few minutes visiting the two churches, which are within sight of each other, and both are interesting. One is in Eastleach Turville, one in Eastleach Martin, they show that the villages were once separate in ownership and allegiance.

*Keble's Clapper Bridge, Eastleach*

## Quenington

Do stop for a while at Quenington. The doorways are very crisp and do not look over 800 years old. The tympanum over the north door shows the defeat of the devil. He is tied up, which allows three souls in danger to escape; one from the grave, one from the sea and one from the devils own mouth. The south door is less frightening, depicting the Coronation of the Virgin. The current art that I always feel has the nearest style to these carvings is the yearly harvest loaves that good bakers still produce. I can imagine the typanums here being made of varnished bread.

The village is well looked after; the large bushes and hedges always seem just back from the hairdressing salon.

# 16. 'Railways, Canals and a Man-eating Monster'

**Brief Description:** A flatter ride which visits some of the attractions to the east of Malmesbury, it can be started either from Malmesbury itself, or from Kemble station on the Swindon to Worcester line.

You can visit the source of the Thames, or at least the main contender for this honour, pass the tunnel entrance to the disused Severn Thames canal and spend some time at the gardens at Rodmarton Manor. Also, allow time for the exploration of Malmesbury.

**Distance:** 31 miles/50 kms – The short cut from Oaksey reduces this to 24 miles/39 kms.

**Terrain:** This is a flatter ride, without a climb, around the plateau of the southern Cotswolds. The difference between the high and low points is only 200 feet/60 metres!

**Rail Access:** The route passes through Kemble which has a station on the London-Swindon-Cheltenham line.

**Links With:** Malmesbury is also the start and finish point for the ride to the west via Owlpen. At Kemble and Coates you are within 3 miles of Cirencester, the base for another two routes.

**Cutting It Short:** As this is a round ride, it is not easy to shorten it. You could cut the loop in half by turning left through Oaksey, joining the return route at Culkerton.

## Route

We begin this route from outside the Tourist Information Centre in Malmesbury. At the Tourist office, pedal into the square of Cross Hayes, and follow the one way roads into the High Street. Turn right into Oxford Street. In a quarter of a mile you cross the river and then turn

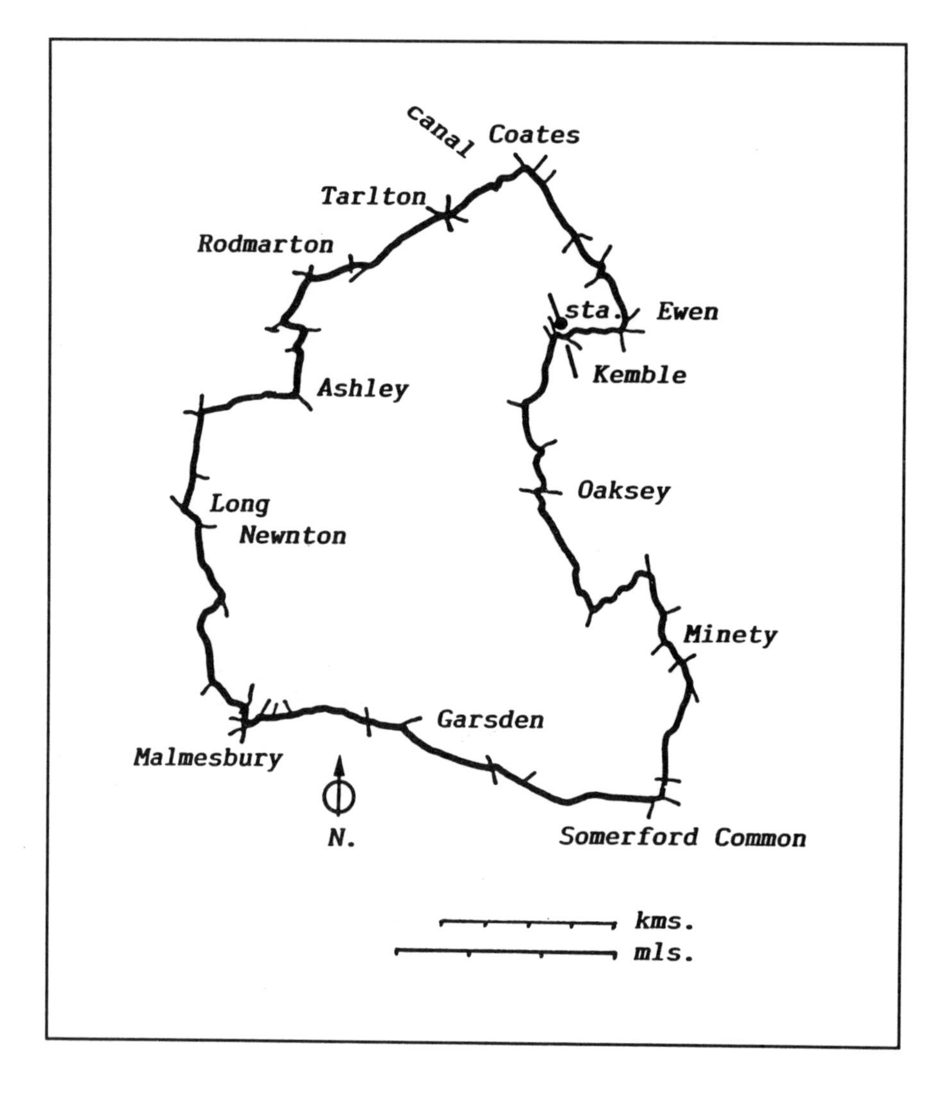

right into Blicks Hill. Cross the 'A' road, with CARE, into the continuation of this lane (ignore any 'No Through Road' signs!) which brings you to Milbourne, by the 'phone box, in a few hundred yards. Continue ahead for 1 mile to a crossroads at which you go ahead to Garsdon, passing the church, before turning right at the 'phone box. After 1.25 miles turn left and immediately right, to cycle on with woods on your left. Ignore a left turn at the end of the wood, and continue for 2 miles to reach an offset crossroads by Somerford Common.

Turn left here, leaving the Common behind you. Go ahead at a crossroads after a quarter of a mile and cycle on for just over 1 mile towards Minety. Take the first left, cross the B4040 after a quarter of a mile, and continue into the village. In Minety bear left and then turn right, to head for Lower Moor which you reach in half a mile having passed under the railway. Go left in the village, parallel with the railway line, before bearing right. After half a mile, turn first left, with a farm to your right. After a quarter of a mile you cross the railway, and in another half mile you reach Upper Minety, with the church on your left. The village lies ahead, but to continue take the first right, reaching Oaksey in 1.5 miles. Turn right by the church and then first left to leave the village. Continue for half a mile, before taking the first proper left turn (not the track to Dean Farm). Continue for 1.5 miles, ignoring a left after half a mile, and having crossed over the railway again. Fine views of Kemble church spire lead you to the village.

You pass the church as you enter Kemble; the village centre and the station are ahead of you, but to continue take the first right by the church, right in only 200 yards and then first left to head for Ewen. You reach Ewen in just under 1 mile, where you turn first left and then first left again. After half a mile you cross under a disused railway and by the course of the Thames and Severn canal. From here it is 400 yards to a junction with the A429. Here you turn right, with CARE, and then first left after 200 yards, by the remains of the canal bank. After half a mile you reach another 'A' road, the A433, which you go straight across. (The source of the Thames is a quarter of a mile left here, and can also be reached by taking a footpath to the left, in just over half a mile ahead of you). Having left the 'A' road behind, you reach Coates in 1.25 miles. Continue until you reach the first left; the church lies a few hundred yards ahead, the village to your right.

To continue from Coates take the left turn, and in half a mile you pass under the railway. The Thames and Severn canal entrance and pub are to your right immediately after the bridge. Continue for half a mile, and a slight climb, to reach Tarlton, going ahead at the first junction by the village green and then keeping left by the (traditional Cotswold concrete) water tower. One and a half miles later you enter Rodmarton, by some odd topiary which seems to be of two Daleks. Turn right by a stone bus shelter, to pass the church, and go ahead (left and right) at an offset crossroads in 200 yards.

Cycle on for half a mile and turn left. Windmill Tump is clear, surrounded by fence and wall, and with several large trees, in the field to your left after this turn. Continue for 1 mile, passing Trull House with good chimneys on your right to reach the A433. Turn left onto this not too busy 'A' road for a quarter of a mile before taking the first, sharp, right (CARE) into a lane through the old railway line. The old line, which ran to Tetbury, is very clear here. At Culkerton turn left at the triangular green and up to the crossroads, and then right signed Ashley. Pass some fine barns to left and right, reaching Ashley in half a mile. Pass a duckpond and turn right by the 'phone box, to continue. The excellent church and manor and farm are a few yards ahead at this point.

Continue from Ashley for a flat 1.25 miles, before taking the first left. Cycle on for a further 1.5 miles, passing the quite isolated church at Long Newnton on your left after 1.25 miles. At the B4014 turn left, and follow this sometimes busy 'B' road for just over 1 mile, before taking the first right. Cycle with a stream on your right for half a mile to enter Brokenborough, passing Rose and Crown. Keep left through the village, gaining fine views of Malmesbury Abbey ahead, and then turn left in half a mile, having crossed a bridge over a stream. Cycle on with this stream on your left for a quarter of a mile; turn left at the first junction, and after 400 yards at a mini-roundabout, turn right to re-enter the centre of Malmesbury by way of Gloucester Road.

## Malmesbury

Malmesbury is the oldest borough in England. The abbey church is wonderful, while the range of the clerics and learned people add to the interest. Oliver or Elmer, 'the flying monk', made his name in 1005 by flying from the west tower of the Abbey, and surviving, despite breaking both legs. Quite what separates 'flying' from a simple plunge from the top of a tower I'm not sure, though one source says that he covered over 620 feet with his strap-on wings. One of the exhibits in the Athelstan Museum is a Whitbread sign for a pub called 'The Flying Monk.'

The Danish invaders pushed as far west and inland as Malmesbury, destroying the original wooden Abbey by fire in 850. The Norman abbey was built for the Benedictine monks, but with the dissolution of the monasteries, the crown agreed to sell it for £1,500. John Leyland, writing in the 1550's, describes his visit to Malmesbury: 'The hole logginges of the abbay be now longging to one Stumpe, an exceding riche clothiar that boute them of the king. This Stumpe was the chief causer and contributor to have the abbay chirch made a paroch chirch. At this present tyme every corner of the vaste houses of office that belongid to the abbay be full of lumbes to weve clooth yn, and this Stumpe entendith to make a stret or 2 for clothiar in the bak vacant ground of the abbay that is within the town walls.'

William Stumpe thus saved the abbey by turning many of its associated buildings into workshops. As a sop to the town he allowed the nave of the abbey to be used as the parish church. A smart operator indeed, Mr.Stumpe. Only five years after the dissolution of the monasteries he was running a business in the former church property.

The well-known hymn 'There is a green hill far away' contains the line 'without a city wall' which means outside the city wall, not that it did not have a city wall. The remains of the 13th. century church in Bird Cage Walk is called St.Paul Without in the same way. This was the parish church that Stumpe so 'generously' replaced.

## Oaksey

This comfortable and still working village has a fine buildings, including a good church from the 1200s which contains a wall painting of Christ and the Trades, designed to show the early worshippers that salvation could be achieved only by hard work. A predecessor of the Protestant work ethic perhaps? As you leave the village and turn right after half a mile, to your left you will see the clear mound of a Norman 'Motte and Bailey', known as Norwood Castle.

## Kemble

Just to show that nimby-ism (Not-In-My-Back-Yard) is not new, Kemble was the site of a battle over the coming of the railway. Local landowners, the Gordon family, were so horrified at the idea of a train being visible from their land that they not only demanded £7,000 compensation, but also insisted on a totally unnecessary 'tunnel', which is still used today.

## Coates

The church at Coates lies a few hundred yards ahead of you as you turn left to pass the canal entrance. You reach it by a nice path between two good houses; the garden of the right-hand house is well kept and is protected by a large carved warthog. It is worth the short detour even if just to gaze at the ghastly anthropophagus or man eater. This is a carving up on the tower. The 'thing' has already eaten the top half of its human meal, and is about to get to the crunchy bit. Worth a look, but maybe not a lunch stop . . .

## Thames and Severn Canal

What a wonder this must have been. When it was finished in 1789 even the 'Thunderer', The Times newspaper, described it as a 'stupendous achievement'. The concept was simple: to link the two most important lines of transport in the region, the Rivers Thames and Severn, by canal. This would open up new markets and reduce the cost and time taken to transport goods. For much of its length it needed to be built upwards, and the some sections that you can still see look more like a railway embankment than a canal trench. The major achievement of the whole project was the tunnel, the eastern entrance to which this route passes. We can only imagine the hard work, danger and discomfort that the navigators or 'navvies' had to put up with while they built it. They must have been many months over the work since the pub by the entrance was originally built to serve them. The surveyors must also have been skilled men to drive the two mile cutting through solid limestone so precisely.

It was partly this limestone that later caused problems with the canal; the porous stone leaked terribly. The Great Western Railway, which was competition for the waterways, arrived later and was built within a few yards of the canal, and the general decline in the use of the waterways accelerated. The G.W.R. bought the canal in 1876 to prevent a rival railway building a track along the level course of the navigation. The tunnel was officially closed in 1911; the last journey through the tunnel was made in 1933.

Ernest Temple Thurston was writing the 'Flower of Gloster' just before the canal was closed. This told the story of his narrowboat travels throughout Central England on 'The Flower'. He must have made one of the last journeys through the tunnel:

> *"What did the leggers used to be paid?" I asked after the first mile, when it seemed all sensation had gone out of my limbs and they were working merely in obedience to the despairing effort of my will.*
>
> *"Five shillings, sir, for a loaded boat. Two and six for an empty one".*
>
> *I groaned.*
>
> *"A pound wouldn't satisfy me" I said.*
>
> *"No, sur, I suspects not. It's always easier to do these things for nothing".*
>
> *For an hour that was all we said. For an hour I legged away, thinking how true that casual statement was – 'It's always easier to do these things for nothing'. It is – always. All labour would be play if it were not for payment.*
>
> *But one does not think of this sort of thing for long while legging it through the Sapperton Tunnel. A drip of shiny water on one's face is quite enough to upset the most engrossing contemplation. I saw the pin-point of light growing to a pin's head, and we still laboured on, only resting a few minutes to light a fresh piece of candle or take breath.*
>
> *It was evening when we came out into the light again and, though the sun had set, with shadows falling everywhere it almost dazzled me. A barge in the next lock rose above the lock's arms, with every line cut out against the pale sky".*

## Rodmarton

The manor house at Rodmarton was built between 1909 and 1926. It was an 'Arts and Crafts' building, and constructed carefully using the principles of this movement. The church is of an unusual shape and looks rather like one you might find in the Swiss Alps.

Under a mile past the village, to your left, is Windmill Tump, protected by a fence and a wall. There are tall trees growing round its edge. Though there is no footpath shown on the map access is allowed at 'any reasonable time'. It is a Neolithic (New Stone) long barrow and lies east to west so that the sun rose, and still rises, at one end of the structure and sets at the other. One chamber was found to hold the bodies of ten adults and three children. Nevertheless, it makes a fine place for a break!

*Sapperton Tunnel, South-East Portal*

## Ashley

The tiny village of Ashley is well worth a pause from your pedalling. The land here is flat; just a mile to the east is the course of the Fosse Way which the Romans drove across the plain. The manor house and farm buildings sit happily by the church.which has a Norman tympanum and a steep roof made from Cotswold tiles. The manor and barns are Cotswold classics with dovecote holes, complete with doves, and by the barn next to the drive there is a mounting block to help you up on to your horse. The gardens of the manor are sometimes open to the public as part of the National Gardens scheme.

The church itself is dedicated to St.James. Ashley is mentioned in the Doomsday Book, but not its church, which was however built by 1160. The arch and tympanum date from this period and are decorated with simple patterns rather than dramatic carvings. Outside do look at the small west window in the bell tower. The lintel over the opening is made from a stone coffin lid. Why waste good stone? There is a very well-researched guide to the history of Ashley, and its buildings, available inside the church.

# 17. 'Two Hidden Valleys and a Glimpse of the Sea'

**Brief Description:** This is a longer ride and if you want time to examine and explore, you'll need to take a couple of days over it. Though you can avoid the loop that takes in Owlpen it's a perfect cluster of buildings, in a lovely situation. On the western part of the ride, you are to the far west of the Cotswolds themselves, just on the brink of the break in the hills, before the country flattens out into the Vale of Berkeley, and the Severn estuary. You may get glimpses of the sea at a couple of points on this route.

This is a generally prosperous part of the country, even rich. The ancestral piles and the dwellings of the royal family keep the money moving around here. You can take in visits to several manor houses and the arboretum at Westonbirt with its collection of over 13,000 trees and shrubs.

**Distance:** 48 miles/77 kms – Avoiding the Owlpen loop reduces this by 5 miles.

**Terrain:** From Malmesbury and northwest towards Owlpen you are on the flat and high tops of the plateau. Around Wotton-under-Edge, and as you swing south along the western stretch of the ride you have several descents and subsequent climbs where the streams pour off the plateau and head for the sea to the west. Bearing eastwards again to head back to Malmesbury the country flattens out once more.

**Rail Access:** The nearest stations are at Kemble or Stroud, both on the London-Swindon-Cheltenham line.

**Links With:** Malmesbury is also the starting point for the Coates and Kemble route. At Owlpen and Uley you are just 1.5 miles away from Nympsfield on the Stroud ride.

**Cutting It Short:** Another round route which is designed to make a longer trip and not easy to shorten. You can leave out the loop at Owlpen, which avoids some climbing.

## Route

We start this ride from outside the Tourist Information Centre in Malmesbury.

With your back to the Tourist centre proceed into the square of Cross Hayes, right into St.Dennis Lane and then follow the High Street round. Pass the mirror, turning left into the B4040, Bristol Street. After 200 yards you should turn left into Dark Lane crossing the bridge over the River Avon. Continue for 2 miles, with the river in the valley to your right. At the tiny village of Foxley you pass the church and then continue, ignoring the left turn by which you will return at the end of the ride, cycling ahead for just under 1 mile to a crossroads. Turn right here and in 1 mile you reach Easton Grey. You cross the river, turn left after the church onto the B4040, and after 300 yards turn right, with care. Cycle on for 2 miles. During the later part of this section you will pass the grounds of Westonbirt School on your left. When you reach a crossroads with the A433, the entry to Westonbirt Arboretum is 400 yards to your left. To continue you should go straight across the 'A' road. Cycle on ahead for 3 miles to a crossroads with the 'A46' where you cross straight over, with care, and continue for just over half a mile when you take the first left by the first building on this road. Your route then wiggles right/left/right into the combe and then climbs out of it to pass the church of Newington Bagpath.

Continue from Newington Bagpath for half a mile, passing good barns, to a small 'T' junction where you turn right to reach the A4135 in half a mile, by a pub. Cross the 'A' road with care, (it's really left and immediately right), to head for Kingscote, which you reach in a quarter of a mile. Take the first left at the village, though the church is to your right, to a 'T' junction in half a mile. Turn right at the 'T' to arrive at a broad junction with the B4058 in a quarter of a mile. Turn left onto the 'B' road, which you follow for a quarter of a mile before turning right at the crossroads. Take the small right turn after a few hundred yards to head for Owlpen.

[When visiting Owlpen you have a choice. You can either cycle on for as far as you need to see the hamlet in all its glory and then simply retrace your route. To find the best viewpoint, continue only as far as the small house on the right, after 300 yards, where the lane swings left.

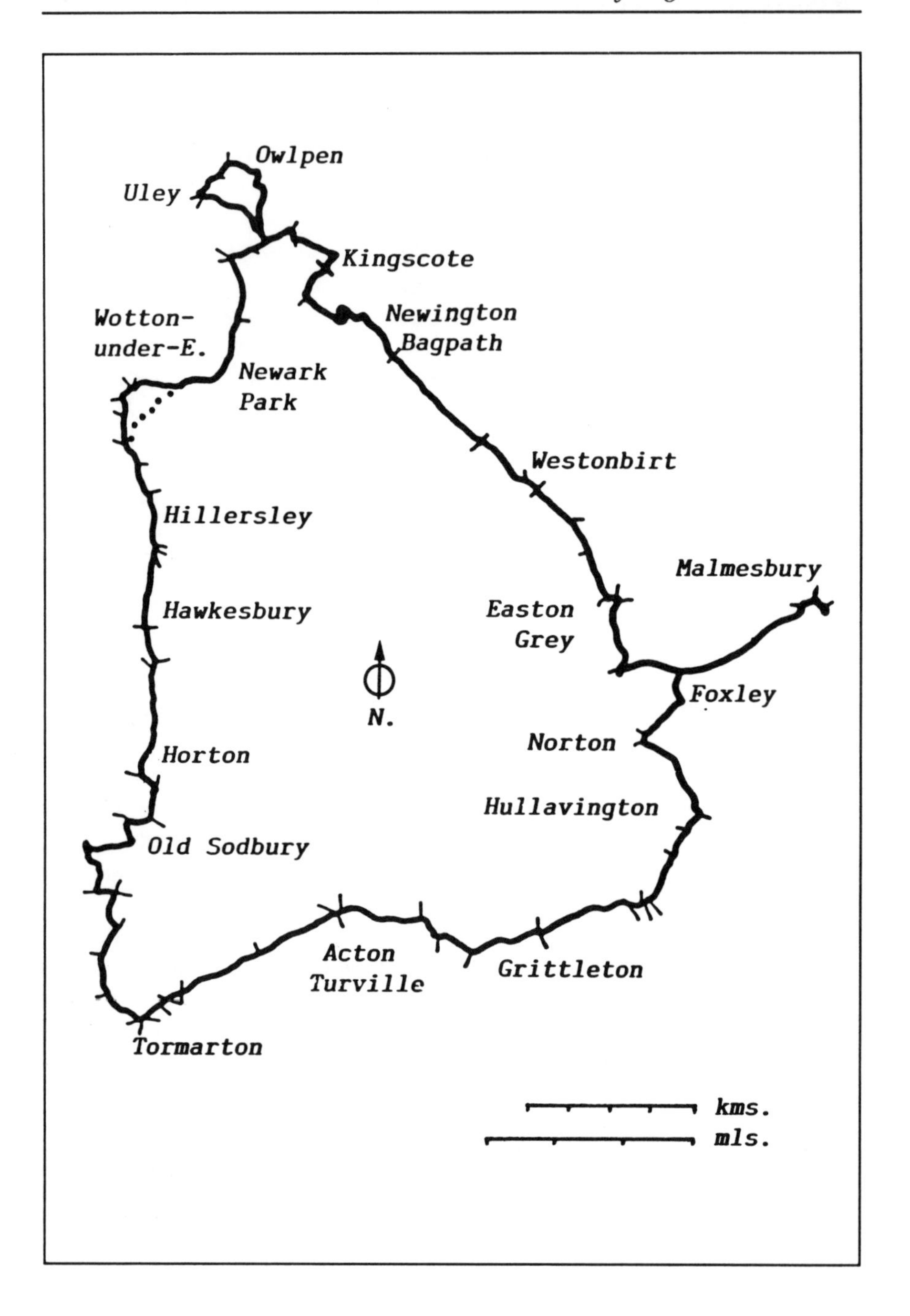
Owlpen
Uley
Kingscote
Wotton-
under-E.
Newington
Bagpath
Newark
Park
Westonbirt
Hillersley
Malmesbury
Hawkesbury
Easton
Grey
N.
Foxley
Norton
Horton
Hullavington
Old Sodbury
Acton
Turville
Grittleton
Tormarton
kms.
mls.

Alternatively you can cycle right through Owlpen, 'Unsuitable for Motors', turning left after 1 mile onto the B4066 to head through Uley, turning left again after half a mile, to return to your starting point for this loop, in 1 mile. This option will require considerable climbing. You'll see the extent of this from the viewpoint mentioned above.]

Having seen Owlpen, or even having decided not to, you'll be (back) at the junction with the B4058. With your back towards Owlpen turn right to follow the 'B' road for 250 yards. You then arrive at a tricky junction with the A4135. You need to turn right onto the 'A' road at this angled turn. You may wish to walk across before remounting, and cycling on for 400 yards. The 'A' road bears right here; the B4058 goes straight ahead; you want to turn left down the lane, at the original metal sign 'Ozleworth $2^1/_2$ miles'.

Cycle on this quiet lane for under 1 mile, with views over to the sea, then you bear right at the ugly tower. For the small detour to Newark park you should bear left at the tower, bearing right at two further junctions to pass the entrance to the Park. To continue to Wotton-under-Edge simply cycle ahead for 2.5 miles. Just before the steep descent begins there is a further option of a track and bridle-path route to save your height, avoiding the drop into the town. This path is clearly signed to the left as the descent begins. It will bring you to the route again, just before Wortley. It is excellent for an off road cycle or if you are used to this sort of 'rough stuff'.

Otherwise, to continue, you drop very quickly (CARE) into Wotton-under-Edge.

The churches and some other attractions in Wotton-under-Edge are further into the village. To continue, you turn left at the first crossroads when you enter the village, and then left after 250 yards, just before the Full Moon pub, to ride round the edge of the hill. Continue to Wortley, which you reach in less than 1 mile. Alderley appears in half a mile, having climbed up and down to cross a small stream in the valley bottom. Pass Alderley church, followed by a quick descent, to reach Hillersley in half a mile. Pass grocers and The Fleece, and continue through the village. Bear right, downhill, as you leave the Hillersley. After one mile you reach a crossroads, where you go ahead, to reach Hawkesbury, by the church, in half a mile. Turn right at the church, which has a set of green dice hedges around it and then bear left after 100 yards, continuing for 1 mile to reach Horton Court and church.

Having looked around, cycle on for half a mile to a 'T' junction. The village of Horton is a little to your right, but our route goes left, round the attractive school, climbing and then bearing right at a junction after 400 yards, and reaching another 'T' junction in half a mile. Here you turn right and downhill to reach Little Sodbury in half a mile. Turn left around the church. In half a mile the road turns right; if you want to inspect the hill fort a footpath leads up to it from this point. Continue for just over half a mile before taking the first left turn. This lane does a double 'dogleg' before arriving at the A432 after 1 mile. Here you should turn left, with CARE, taking the first right after 300 yards, with even more CARE, signed Coombes End. Continue for half a mile to Coombes End where you turn right, but not down the 'No Through Road'.

After 1 mile of cycling with the grounds of Doddington House to your left you reach the B4065. Turn left here to immediately reach a junction with the A46. Cross the 'A' road, with care, into a lane opposite, to pass a pub after 100 yards. Continue for 3 miles, though if you wish to visit Tormarton, church/ other pub, take any of the first four (!) right turns. At Acton Turville you effectively go straight through the village, though this may feel like 'bear right and second right', to head for Littleton Drew which you reach after 1 mile. Bear right through the village, passing the church on your right, and then turn left, to cycle parallel with the motorway. Turn left in a quarter of a mile, with the motorway ahead. (The track to the left here is on the course of the Roman Fosse Way).

After 1 mile you reach a crossroads at Grittleton where you go ahead, passing the pub, and the church, with its four turrets, and then continue for 2 miles, ignoring turns and going ahead at a crossroads after 1.25 miles, to arrive at Hullavington. Cycle through the village, passing the church and pub, to arrive at a crossroads, consisting of three roads and a track ahead. Turn left here, cycling under the railway after 250 yards. 1 mile of level riding brings you to Norton. Here you turn right (ford) and then bear right after a few yards, to pass The Vine Tree pub. Turn left at a small 'T' after half a mile, and in a quarter of a mile you will reach Foxley, the village you cycled through near the start of the ride. Turn right at Foxley, and 2 miles pleasant cycling will bring you back into Malmesbury.

## Malmesbury

There is much to see in Malmesbury, so allow time to explore before you pedal off, or when you return. Some other details are included in the other ride based on the town.

Do inspect the market cross. John Leyland's description from his visit in the 1550's would be at home in any current guide book, with some changes in the spelling . . .

> *"There is a right fair and costely poiece of worke in the market place made al of stone and curiously voultid for poore market folkes to stande dry when rain cummith. Ther be 8 great pillers and 8 poen arches: and the work is 8 square: one great piller in the middle berith up the voulte. The men of the toun made this peace of work in hominum memoria".*

The Athelstan Museum is just round the corner from the Tourist office, in Cross Hayes. It has a good selection of items from Malmesbury and around, including an inn sign of the Flying Monk. You'll also be attracted by the collection of bicycles. One is a tricycle, mainly of wood, which was powered by feet in stirrups and arms. If you are getting tired even on your multi-geared modern wonder, just think of riding a few miles on this wooden 'barrow', as trikes are called, and you'll feel immediately refreshed.

## Easton

The village of Easton Grey has a Georgian Manor house. The seven spanned and solid bridge over the Avon is a good spot at which to stop, look for fish and play Pooh sticks, before you pedal on.

## Newington Bagpath

This is one of my favourite places, and is all the more exciting because it is so unexpected. You've been cycling along flat and high land for seven or eight miles. At many points, often hidden in the trees, you can see large water towers which are essential on the dry plateau. Then a small turn and a bend in the road bring you to a tiny lost valley with a gushing stream. You can see why the houses have clustered the water source for hundred of years, sheltered also from the wind. Hiding in the trees on the far side of the combe is the church of Newington Bagpath, originally built by the Normans. This is now officially redundant; its windows are boarded over and a sign asks that no more is taken from the building.. Some of the innards have been moved to neighbouring churches. It is still a spiritual place. At least one of the graves in the bramble-filled graveyard is still cared for. Others have a crop of daffodils every spring. As you pedal away the valley and church disappear, leaving you to wonder whether you really saw them at all. There is an excellent barn to your left, just after the hamlet.

## Owlpen

Owlpen is hidden away in an almost closed valley. Apart from a few unobtrusive telegraph poles, many views of this cluster of buildings are little different to the way they would have been centuries ago. The village, gathered around a Tudor manor house, includes a Court house and a great barn. The church is slightly separate from the other buildings and shrouded by trees. It has been mostly rebuilt, quite sensitively, but the font is Norman and some of the brasses are Tudor.

The Manor has a complicated history of rebuilding, additions, demolitions and abandonment. Marjery Ollepen, whose family gave the village its name married into the Daunt family in 1464, and the Daunts money allowed embellishment and expansion for over 300 years. From 1850 until 1926 the house was left empty, the Victorians wanting more 'modern' comfort which they found in the nearby Owlpen House, which itself is now demolished. In 1926 Norman Jewson, an architect who improved and restored many Cotswold buildings, took over the Manor and began its repair. He eventually ran out of money, and the east wing that he built was demolished in 1964.

If you visit Owlpen in the spring you won't need to be told about the daffodils which would satisfy a dozen Wordworths. So I won't!

## Ozleworth Bottom

You may have heard of a bird called the Ring Ouzel, a member of the blackbird family. The name Ozleworth comes from the Saxon for a blackbird that lives around the farm.

The tight valleys around here are known as bottoms because they are . . . at the bottom. Most of the streams are now drying up having been taken away by the water companies further upstream. The Little Avon must have been a powerful force as there used to be over a hundred mills in the valley.

## Newark Park

You'll see the signs for Newark Park before you swoop into the valley and reach Wotton-under-Edge. It is only a few hundred yards off your route to the left and worth a visit to make the most of the height you have here. In a lovely position, beside the woods, the house was originally built as an Elizabethan hunting lodge, using stone from the dismantled abbey at Kingswood and even from other local churches and monuments. It was later 'modernised' in 1790; battlements and other impressive features were added to create a home suitable for a wealthy clothing manufacturer. It is more lived in, and less 'precious', than many houses that are open to the public. Opening is limited. Details from 0453 842644.

## Wotton-Under-Edge

In the town itself you'll discover that Wotton really is under the edge of the Cotswold ridge. The Ram Inn (no longer an inn I'm afraid) is a very solid building, partly below street level. It was probably built to accommodate the masons and other workers who built the church of St.Mary the Virgin in the 1200s.

Another church in the village, the Tabernacle in Tabernacle Street, houses a perfect replica of the Roman pavement found at Woodchester, and other local finds. It is open from 10am to 6pm.

At several locations in Wotton-under-Edge you'll see the town's coat of arms. It consists of a sheep and a teasel; the sheep is to be expected in a Cotswold town, while the teasel was used to comb and raise the nap of the cloth made from the wool.

## Hawkesbury

Hawkesbury church, St.Mary's, is in a lovely situation, and makes a good spot for a peaceful break from your pedalling. The doorway is Norman and has a dogtooth decoration rather than the beakheads often seen elsewhere. We still use a similar dogtooth decoration on fabrics.

*The Ram Inn, Wotton-under-Edge*

Above the village you may glimpse the Somerset monument. Lord Edward Somerset fought at the Battle of Waterloo and was formally thanked by Parliament. As he also came from the Beaufort family from Badminton, when he died a very large monument was expected. If you are feeling very fit and keen you can cycle up the ridge, and then walk up to and up the tower. The views are as good as you would anticipate: the Tyndale tower, and the less interesting B.T. mast at Ozleworth, which you passed earlier, are clear to the north, and you can see the Welsh hills if the weather is right.

## Horton

Horton church is nicely placed by a bend in the lane, and butts right up against the neighbouring house. What is the being on the top of the tower? A dragon? Something or somebody on horseback?

Horton Court is something special in that is not a church, though it has a religious history, yet it still has Norman sections. The north wing was built in about 1140, with the rest of the building dating from 1521. The ambulatory enabled people to wander back and forth while earnestly discussing affairs of state without getting wet. The design was brought from Italy by William Knight, who had seen it used there while he was on business for Henry VIII in 1527.

On your left, as you cycle past the village of Horton you can see the clear outline of a hill-fort. This is Iron Age in origin, univallate, meaning it has one ditch (uni is one, vallum from the Latin, where we get our word valley). According to one source parts of the limestone stonework are reddened by fire. One wonders what tragedy overtook the people who made their camp here all those years ago.

## Tormarton

The village is a little close to the busy roads to be tranquil. Do visit the church to see the ghastly memorial to a Lord of the Manor here in the 1600s. Edward Topp is remembered by a sculpture of a severed arm being clutched around its wrist by a mailed fist, all in bloody detail.

## Tormarton

The village is a little close to the busy roads to be tranquil. Do visit the church to see the ghastly memorial to a Lord of the Manor here in the 1600s. Edward Topp is remembered by a sculpture of a severed arm being clutched around its wrist by a mailed fist, all in bloody detail.

## Foxley

This tiny hamlet feels very quiet and isolated. There has been a settlement here since before the Doomsday Book, in which Foxley is called 'Foxelege'. The first rector was William De La Mare in 1334. His patron was John De La Mare, which sounds like more than just coincidence. The nearby hamlet of Bremilham was a separate parish and still has its own church, built in Cowage farmyard! You'll pass the farm on your left as you cycle back towards Malmesbury. The poll tax register in 1377 showed 31 people paying tax in Bremilham and only 12 in Foxley. This must mean that most of the two hamlets has simply disappeared. A nearby, and now bare, mound is still called Mansion Hill, and this may give a clue as to where some of the original settlement used to be.

# 18. 'Strutting Stroud'

**Brief Description:** A ride of two halves! One half is very flat, using a cyclepath created from a disused railway track, but near two stations, at Stroud and Stonehouse, which are still in use, and make good start points. Once you leave the cyclepath, there is a short but quite steep climb out of the valley of the Nailsworth Stream. This leads you onto a tithe barn, a gem of a church, remains of a Roman Road, and by a Bronze Age burial chamber. The final section is again along a cyclepath.

**Distance:** 17 miles/27 kms.

**Terrain:** The cycle track on the disused railway is as level and gradual as you'd expect; there are some barriers at junctions where you will have to dismount. From Nailsworth there is a short climb, but the views from the ridge that you reach makes it very worth while. You then make the best of your height, before winding into the valley by Stonehouse.

Most of the surface of the cycle path is of compacted stone, not tarmac, but is generally in good condition. If you do find it bumpy try cycling just at the edge of the path where the start of the soil evens out the gaps between the stones. There is one section of bridlepath by Hetty Pegler's Tump. This is short, downhill, and is accompanied by lovely views.

**Rail Access:** The route is based on Stroud Station. Stonehouse Station, on the same line, is by the western end of the cycle path.

**Links With:** Owlpen and Uley, on the ride westwards from Malmesbury, are within 1.5 miles of Nympsfield. Kemble Station is the next one towards Swindon from Stroud; this could be used to join the other Malmesbury ride at Kemble.

**Cutting It Short:** Having made the ascent to Nympsfield it is a pity to waste your height, but you could return to the start point on the cycletrack at Stroud straight down the B4066. We show a choice of descents from the summit, one of which cuts out the section through Coaley, saving a few miles.

## Route

We start this ride from Stroud Station. There is parking nearby.

From the station you have only 200 yards of cycling on normal roads in the centre of Stroud! You could hardly have a neater way out of a town centre.

Leave the station by the town centre side, to pass the elegant 'Imperial Hotel'. At the 'T' junction turn left to go under the railway. At the mini-roundabout go ahead to pass 'The Bell' and head downhill along the marked cycle lane to pass through the subway under the main road. Continue on the cycle lane on the left-hand pavement, climbing slightly for 100 yards, before turning sharp left to go through the cycle barrier and reach the start of this section of dis-used railway track. Turn right to cycle under the two good bridges. Continue until you reach a grey stone bridge; here you can either go ahead and then slither down the bank, or bear left up the path to the road. Assuming you are not a slitherer, at the road turn right and then left after a few yards around 'The Railway' pub. Turn right, with care, after 100 yards into a cycle path at the edge of the new estate. Go ahead into a second cycle path, over a stream, and then follow a third cycle sign to reach the signed three-way junction on the railway path.

Turn left here, signed 'Woodchester', though you will arrive from the right at this point on your return. You now essentially continue for 4 miles to reach Nailsworth. You will have some cycle barriers to tackle. At a couple of points the path is quite noisy, at others it runs through industrial estates. These were originally set up to be served by the railway of course. Do notice the well built personal underpasses under the trackbed. I like the minature, beautifully engineered, steel bridge that still takes you over the stream, but which is now in the middle of a housing estate!

At Nailsworth you will see the original 'Railway Hotel' sign ahead of you. Before cycling on, have a glance at the station building on the bank to your left. Continue up to the hotel (which isn't one any more) and turn right. Cross the stream and then turn left at the 'T' junction to reach a mini-roundabout after a few yards where you turn right, with care, into Spring Hill.

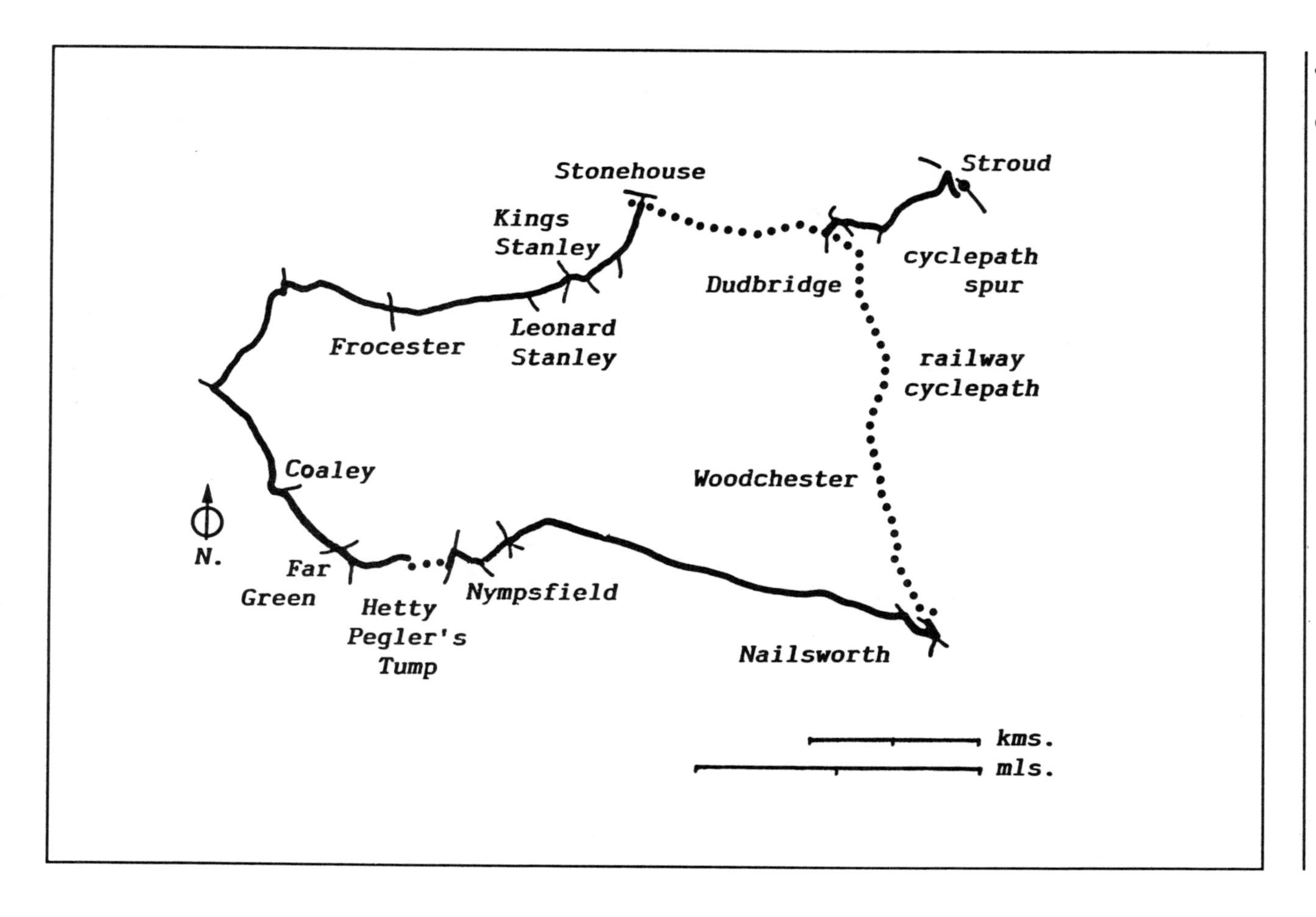
Stonehouse
Stroud
Kings Stanley
cyclepath spur
Dudbridge
Frocester
Leonard Stanley
railway cyclepath
Coaley
Woodchester
N.
Far Green
Hetty Pegler's Tump
Nympsfield
Nailsworth
kms.
mls.

Continue up hill on this road bearing left past the school on your right for 1 mile. When you pass a larger school, on your left, you have left the outskirts of Nailsworth behind. After a few yards continue/bear left into the lane signed 'Single Track Road'.

After 2 miles of ridge riding with excellent views, you reach the village of Nympsfield. Go ahead at the offset crossroads (the village centre and pub are to your left), turning right at the 'T' junction in half a mile.

On reaching the B4066 you should turn left to visit the Tump a quarter of a mile away, and then return to this juction. You then have a choice. If you wish to cycle direct to Frocester, go ahead and bear right down the hill, or for the direct 'B' road return to Stroud follow the signs to the north-east. But to continue on the full route turn left for a hundred yards until you see a sign for the Cotswold Way on your right. Cross, with care, and go down this bridlepath. The path is steep to start with, and unless you like mad descents you would do best to walk down through the woods. The gradient then eases and you reach tarmac in a quarter of a mile.

Go ahead at the tarmac, passing the cottages, bearing right after half a mile. On reaching Coaley bear right to pass through the village, passing the church on your right, and the cottages that 'stole' some heads from the church on your left. Turn right just out of the village to pass under the railway in a quarter of a mile. Pass the good house and barns and continue for 1 mile to reach old Frocester church with only its porch and spire remaining. Cross over the railway, with the old station to your right, and cycle on through the village going ahead at the crossroads with the 'Gloucestershire Hussars' on your left. In 1 mile you will come into Leonard Stanley.

The church and pub are to your right, but to continue cycle ahead into Kings Stanley. Bear left through the village at the shops, passing the 'Kings Head' on your right to reach the church ahead. Having inspected the church continue out of the village. Cross the stream by two good mills one of Cotswold stone, the other of brick, and turn right, with care, onto the cyclepath, confusingly signed 'Stonehouse'. Bear right along the cyclepath away from the bridge.

Continue for 2 miles to reach the remains of the station platforms, with a tube tunnel ahead. Cycle through the tunnel to reach the signed threeway junction where you started. Turn left off the cyclepath and follow your outward route to return to Stroud Station.

## Stroud

Stroud had everything to make it one of the centres of the cloth industry. A damp climate which prevented the yarn from breaking, dependable and fast flowing streams to provide power for the mills. There was a source of Fuller's Earth (for use in dyeing) nearby, and teasels, with which to raise the nap on the best quality fabric, grew in the valley.

It became a prosperous town, able to send its top quality cloth throughout the world, using the port of Bristol. Once again, however, the weavers, who often were employed as outworkers, using their own homes as their workplace, saw little of the prosperity. W.A.Miles produced his 'Report and Condition of the Hand Loom Weavers of Gloucestershire' in 1839:

"Many outdoor weavers cannot afford to taste meat; many cannot have tea for breakfast. That meal consists of bread and water with a little salt; it is called 'Tea-Kettle Tea'. A journeyman weaver named William Evans states that breakfast is warm water with a little salt or some pepper in it, and a crust of bread but he cannot have enough of that at times. The dinner of a weaver is generally a piece of bread and cheese, or some potatoes for himself and family, with some fat or 'flick' poured over them."

Things became so bad that the troops were called out in 1825:

> *"At Stroud we found a company of the 10th Hussars: these troops had been summoned a few days ago to assist the civil power in quelling a riotous uprising of the operative weavers. A certain degree of dissatisfaction has existed for some time about wages, which led to dis-orderly assemblages, actual violence and alarming tumult".*

Understatement indeed by Rev.F.E.Witts from Upper Slaughter; the workers must have been in great difficulty to resort to rioting when they saw the odds against them.

## Nailsworth

Nailsworth shows its industrial history. Some of the buildings would look at home in Northern cities such as Manchester.

## Nympsfield

Nympsfield is 700feet above sea level and as you would expect provides some fine views toward the Severn estuary.

## A Cotswold rhyme:

*Nympsfield is a pretty place,*
*Set upon a tump,*
*But all the people do live upon,*
*Is ag pag dump.*

You are unlikely to find Ag Pag Dump on sale now; it was supposedly a suet pudding with sloe berries added, which we only use now for sloe gin. It sounds rather bitter. A friend who lives in the Cotswolds knows it as Pan Ag, which sounds to me like a corruption of Pan Haggarty which you will find in some old recipe books, but this is made from potatoes!

## Coaley

Samuel Rudder published his 'A New History of Gloucestershire' in 1779. Considering he was a local lad, from nearby Uley, his description of Coaley is either very honest or just vindictive:

"The public roads here are the worst that can be conceived; and the poor labouring people are so abandoned to nastiness, that they throw every thing within a yard or two of their doors, where the filth makes a putrid stench, to the injury of their own health, and the annoyance of travellers, if any come among them. The better houses are gone to ruin, and there is not a gentleman resident in the parish".

There was clearly rivalry, and even hatred, between neighbouring villages which perhaps gave Rudder his reason for this piece. Annual events such as the Coaley Wake and the Nympsfield Revels were used by the local rowdy lads as a good excuse for a punch-up. So bad did it get that the magistrates banned the fairs in the 1850s. Things have now improved!

## Frocester

Frocester is on the course of a Roman, and probably even earlier, trackway that ran from Easton Grey near Malmesbury to the crossing of the Severn at Arlingham, onto The Forest of Dean and into Wales. (The route in this guide which covers the west of Malmesbury runs along another section of this road). When most of the original parish church was pulled down in 1952 the remains of a substantial Roman villa were found beneath it, which must have made an important halt on the long journey to and from darkest Wales. No fools these church builders; why waste some perfectly good Roman foundations?

The 180 feet long tithe barn at Frocester is wonderfully preserved and carefully restored. Its construction seems to have been supervised by Abbot John de Gamages, who held his position at Gloucester Abbey between 1284 and 1306. Some of the stone used for the barn may have been taken from the remains of the Roman villa nearby. Barns such as this are called 'tithe' or 'tythe' as they were built to store the grain and other crops demanded by the church landowners as rent. This was based on a tenth of their produce; the word comes from 'teogopian' the Old English for one tenth. The barn is open 'during all reasonable daylight hours'; ring 0453 823250 for details.

## Leonard Stanley and Kings Stanley

These villages run one into the other; estates from each have spread. Leonard Stanley has two churches, one in use as a church, one as a barn! The barn is the remaining part of a Saxon building, which used to be the parish church. The existing church has some perfect, crisp Norman carving. One in particular on a pillar by the altar shows Mary Magdelene washing Christ's feet with her hair, with other little figures hiding round the corner. This was the monk's church, and the fishpond to provide them with fresh food throughout the year can still be seen.

The church at Kings Stanley seems in the centre of the built up village, but just to the north of the churchyard you have good views of the valley and the small tributary of the River Frome. The remains of a moat, probably fed by this stream, are visible in the north-west of the churchyard. A good row of clipped yews leads to the church. As you enter notice the fine carving above the door of St.George, to whom the church is dedicated, on his horse battling with a serrated backed dragon.

Inside the church simply look up! The beautifully-worked, but rather excessive decoration which covers even the tiebeams was completed in 1876. Even more elaborate is the organ which wouldn't be out of place in a fairground. The row of heads about half-way up the current walls are the Norman corbel stones upon which the orignal roof supports were placed.

*Stroudwater Canal, King's Stanley*

# 19. Tower to Tower to Tower; Oxford to Bath

**Brief Description:** This route offers an ideal introduction to the region. If you have just one precious week's holiday, or want to include the Cotswolds in a longer trip through the country, this ride offers a representative taster to the area. Since it passes by or crosses most of the other rides in the guide, you can also incorporate these if you have the time and/or the energy. The title refers to three towers, one in Oxford, one at Broadway and one just outside Bath, that provide markers of your progress, and excellent views. 'Tower to tower to tower' is presented in a more simple style than the other rides, with only brief descriptions of a few sites of interest. Where this ride coincides with other routes in the guide you'll find fuller details contained in that section.

As mentioned elsewhere, exactly where the Cotswolds start and finish is open to question. We have taken the two classic cities of Oxford and Bath as our east and west boundary points. Whether 'officially' in the Cotswolds or not they provide a perfect start and finish for this ride which takes in many of the highlights of the area.

**Distance:** As the crow flies, the distance from Oxford to Bath is just 54 miles/87 kilometres. As the cyclist pedals, however, it is rather different and our selected route totals 156 miles/251 kilometres; the optional northern loop represents 47 miles/75 kilometres of this total. No doubt some 'hard riders' will be happy to do this in one day and still be ready for more. For lesser and probably wiser mortals, and certainly for anyone who wants to see something of the land they are cycling through, I'd suggest that this route is completed over a week or so. The train can be used for the return journey; information on the cyclepath along a disused railway line from Bath to Bristol is included to link up with the more direct and frequent services from Bristol Temple Meads Station.

**Terrain:** The terrain over this route is too variable to sum up. The ride has been chosen to provide a variety of riding. None of the climbs is a real horror, however, and the height you gain is usually lost only gradually. There are two sections of footpath where you must dismount and walk a short way. They both provide useful links and avoid busy roads.

**Safety and Pleasure:** Excepting the city centres at the start and finish of the route there is only 1 mile of 'A' road, made up of small sections, in the whole 156 miles ride!

## Itinerary

**OXFORD,** Cumnor, Appleton, Longworth, Charney Bassett, Goosey, Baulking, Uffington, Fernham, Faringdon, Great Coxwell, Badbury Clump, Buscot House, Kelmscott, Langford, Filkins, Little Barrington, Great Barrington, Little Rissington, Bourton-on-the-Water.

Bourton-on-the-Water, Broadway Tower, Dovers Hill, Ilmington, Darlingscot, Shipston, Wilmington, Cherington, Whichford, Rollright Stones, Cornwell, Kingham, Daylesford, Lower Oddington, Icomb, Little Rissington, Bourton-on-the-Water.

Bourton-on-the-Water, Farmington, Northleach, Coln St.Dennis, Coln St.Rogers, Winson, Ablington, Bibury, Barnsley, Daglingworth, Park Corner, Cherington.

Cherington, Chavenage Green, Kingscote, Newington Bagpath, Leighterton, Didmarton, Little Badminton, Badminton, Acton Turville, Burton, Grittleton, West Kington, Freezing Hill, Lansdown, **BATH.**

## Route Directions:

### SECTION 1: Oxford to Bourton-on-the-Water

We start at Oxford station, but before leaving the city you need to find the first tower. If you prefer to do this on foot, you can leave your cycle at the huge and chaotic cycle park at the station.

There are several towers in Oxford which you can climb to gain a view over the 'dreaming spires', but we have chosen the Saxon tower of St. Michael, and this is about five minutes walk or cycle from the station. It is in Cornmarket Street. Follow the signs to the city centre; left out of the station forecourt, bear left into Hythe Bridge Street, ahead into George Street to reach a crossroads, with Broad Street ahead. Turn right here and St. Michael's is 50 yards on your right, by the junction with Ship Street.

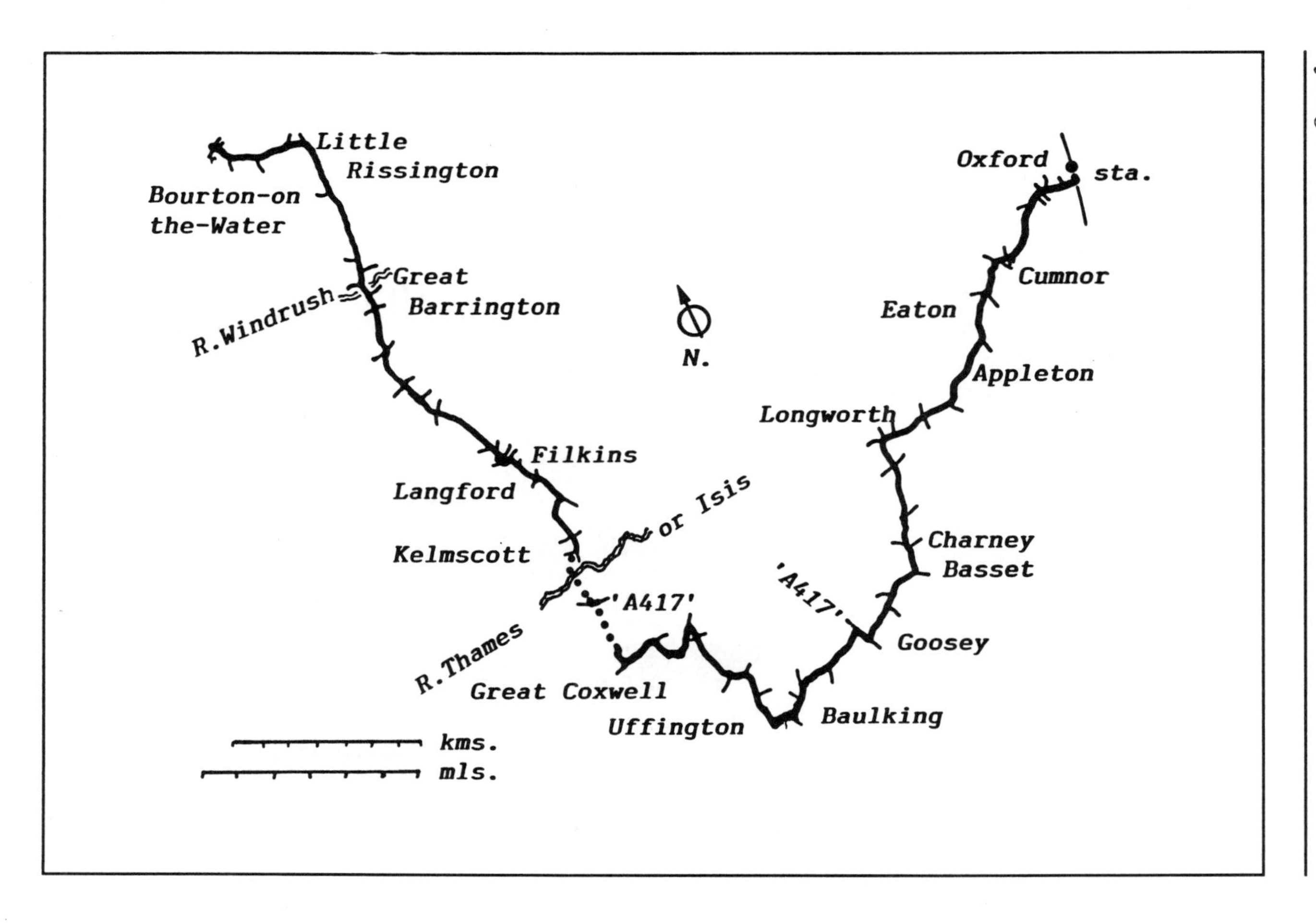
Little
Rissington
Bourton-on
the-Water
Great
Barrington
R. Windrush
N.
Oxford
sta.
Cumnor
Eaton
Appleton
Longworth
Filkins
Langford
Kelmscott
or Isis
Charney
Basset
'A417'
'A417'
Goosey
R. Thames
Great Coxwell
Uffington
Baulking
kms.
mls.

## St. Michael's Tower, Oxford

It costs £1 (in 1993) to go up the tower, and you'll also need some 10 pence pieces to operate the clock mechanism and bells on the way down. Around the parapet of the tower are descriptions of what you can see. If you look west, in the direction of Botley, you'll see the valley that marks your route out of Oxford.

The tower is the oldest structure in Oxford, and once formed part of the city's defences. Inside the church, where William Morris was married, are four figures in stained glass which are the oldest in Oxford and date from c.1290.

*St Michael's Tower, Oxford*

Back at Oxford railway Station, cycle down out of the forecourt to the main road. Turn right under the railway, after 1 mile bear left onto the B4044 under the dual carriageway, bear left after 300 yards. After 1.5 miles pass over the dual carriageway at Cumnor, pass the church on your left, and then turn left for Appleton. In half a mile bear right and then left and continue to reach Appleton in 1 mile. Cycle through the village and cross the A415 in 2 miles. One mile later, turn left to cross the A420 in half a mile. Continue for 2 miles to reach the village of Charney Bassett. Leave the village and turn first right after 1 mile. You reach Goosey in 1.5 miles. Continue through the village to the A417. Here turn right for 400 yards and then turn first left to Baulking, which you reach in 2 miles. Bear left in the village to cross the railway. You arrive in Uffington after one mile.

## Uffington White Horse

This figure cut into the high chalkland is surrounded by other earthworks. Some have mystical connections while others are historical. To the west of White Horse hill is a natural mound called Dragon Hill. This is where St.George is supposed to have killed the poor fire breathing beast. The castle on the top of the hill is an Iron Age earthwork.

One theory about the horse itself is that it was created to celebrate the victory by King Alfred, when he wasn't burning the cakes, over the Danish invaders in 871 AD. In fact, it is about 1000 years older than that. You can cycle up onto the ridge to have a closer look at the horse, but like many very large features you get the best view from a distance. It is a very crisp shape, and 'The Scouring of the White Horse' has been a regular task for hundreds of years.

To continue from Uffington, turn right at the 'T' junction; pass the church, turning right and right again to leave the village. In half a mile you pass under the railway, and then bear first left in a further half a mile to reach Fernham. Join the main road through the village for 300 yards and turn first right to arrive at Little Coxwell in 1.5 miles. Continue to the A420 and take the small lane opposite, into the outskirts of Faringdon; pass the school on your right and at first junction turn sharp left. You arrive at Great Coxwell in 1 mile.

## The Barn at Great Coxwell

This is something special. Descriptions of the barn range from a cathedral built for grain, to an agricultural temple. It was built not for spiritual reasons, but as a practical storehouse; it may be old and beautifully crafted but its modern equivalent is a large warehouse or corrugated iron. grainstore. This barn was one of William Morris's favourite sites; he called it 'the finest piece of architecture in England'.

**Opening**: is at 'any reasonable time' all year round?

To continue, at the crossroads in Great Coxwell village turn right and then left after a quarter of a mile onto the B4019. Pass Badbury Clump on your right and continue downhill to take the first right turn. Cycle on to Brimstone Farm where you should dismount and walk for under half a mile along the footpath. At the next building, Oldfield Farm, you can remount and cycle along the farm track, which is now a bridlepath again. Continue for a quarter of a mile with the grounds of Buscot Park on your left, to reach the A417.

## Buscot House

Though it now appears a classic 'stately home', Buscot Park was the site of an experiment in mechanised farming in the middle of the last century. An Australian bought the land and set up a distillery. He built a railway to collect the sugar beet from the fields, steam powered machines replaced the working horses, a telegraph system made communication around the estate more efficient, and he even made his own artificial fertiliser.

In the house is a excellent collection of paintings; of relevance to the Cotswolds are the works by several of the Pre-Raphaelites including a series by Edward Burne-Jones, who also designed a new stained glass window for the nearby church. The house is administered by the National Trust. It is open from Easter to the end of September, on Wednesday, Thursday and Friday, and on the second and fourth weekends. If this confuses you, details are available from 0367 240786.

To continue, turn left onto the 'A' road in front of the park, and after 300 yards turn right, with CARE, into the entrance of Kilmester's Farm. Dismount as you come out of the wood, as you are now on a footpath, and walk past the farm and then on to the Thames. Cross the river by the footbridge, and follow the footpath on the northern bank to the edge of Kelmscott where you can officially remount.

## Kelmscott Manor

William Morris, who often visited the tower at Broadway which you pass later on this route, made Kelmscott his summer home. You can see why he fell in love with it from the outside; inside is a collection of his varied work. Morris died here in 1896, and was in buried in the church in the village. The Manor is only open for part of the year, and then only regularly on Wednesdays. It can, however, be made available for pre-booked groups.

Details from Mr. Chapman, 0367 52486.

To continue, bear right in Kelmscott and then turn left, away from the river and manor, to reach a crossroads in a quarter of a mile. Go across here and at a 'T' junction after 1 mile, turn left to reach Langford in half a mile. Pass through village with the church on your left and continue to reach Filkins after one mile.

At the first crossroads in Filkins village go ahead, then bear left and first right to pass under the A361. Continue for 2 miles to go ahead at a small crossroads, and continue to a further crossroads in 1 mile. Ahead for a further 1 mile brings you to a crossing of the B4425. Cross straight over here to reach the A40. At this busy road cross over, with CARE, to enter Little Barrington in a quarter of a mile. Continue left through the village before turning right to cross the Windrush and climb up hill into Great Barrington. Continue left, up hill, out of the village, climbing gently, for 3.5 miles. Turn left opposite airfield houses to whiz through Little Rissington to reach Bourton-on-the-Water in 2 miles.

# Section 2: The Northern Loop

If you wish to miss out this upper part of the route, you will need to skip the next section and rejoin the ride at Bourton-on-the-Water, for Section 3.

Leave Bourton-on-the-Water along the main street, to the A429. Turn right, with CARE, and after only 100 yards turn left. Continue, passing the Slaughters on your right after 1 mile and go ahead at a crossroads with the B4068. Continue ahead now for 5 miles, going straight across at no less than five cross roads and ignoring all turns. You will arrive at a small junction at which you turn right, 'Chipping Campden 4'. In 300 yards continue left, 'Broadway 4', to reach views of Broadway Tower ahead once you have cleared the woods.

Pass the tower on your left and continue for half a mile to a broad junction with the A44. Go across here, with CARE, and cycle along the wide lane for half a mile to turn right at the first junction. Cycle downhill for 1 mile, continuing at an offset junction, with Chipping Campden in the vale to your right. Continue downhill to the B4035. Bear left here and then fork right after 200 yards. Turn right off the 'B' road after a further 250 yards. Continue for 2 miles to go ahead at a small crossroads. At a tiny 'T' junction turn right and then left after a quarter of a mile and continue for 2.5 miles into Ilmington.

Cycle into the village before turning right, and ignoring a left turn after 100 yards, to reach a 'T' junction in half a mile. Turn right here, reaching Darlingscott in 1.5 miles. Cycle through the village and in half a mile you arrive at the A429. Cross the 'A' road, with CARE, to approach the centre of Shipston-on-Stour in less than 1 mile.

In Shipston-on-Stour turn left at the 'T' junction and at square junction effectively go ahead to cross the river. At the small crossroads in a quarter of a mile turn right passing by Willington in half a mile. Continue left at a small junction 150 yards after the village. Continue for 1 mile to reach Cherington. Turn first left after crossing over the river and then go ahead at a small offset junction after a quarter of a mile at Stourton. Cycle on for 2 miles to pass straight through Whichford.

Climb out of the village and in a further 1 mile, at an offset crossroads, turn right and cycle along the ridge for 1 mile before turning first right. You will reach the A34 in 1 mile. Cross over at this junction. You pass the Rollright Stones here; continue past stones and after 2 miles you reach the A44. Turn left and right, with CARE, after only 100 yards. 1 mile later you will reach Cornwell, where you turn right to cycle through the village. After 400 yards, at an offset crossroads turn left, to

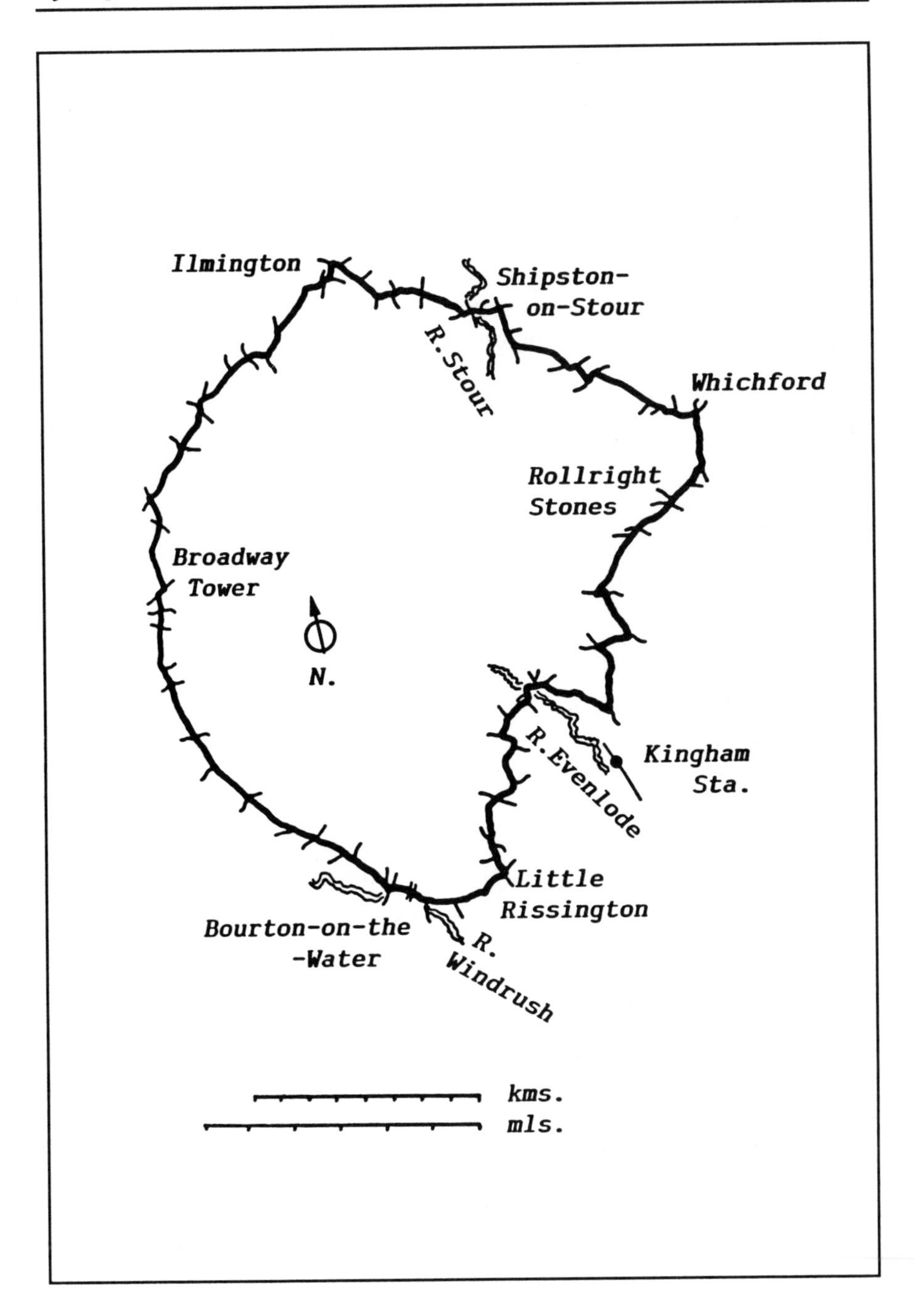
Ilmington
Shipston-
on-Stour
R.Stour
Whichford
Rollright
Stones
Broadway
Tower
N.
Kingham
Sta.
R.Evenlode
Little
Rissington
Bourton-on-the
-Water
R.
Windrush
kms.
mls.

approach Kingham in 1 mile. At the junction before the village turn sharp right.

(If you need to make a speedy return to Oxford, or even wish to start this route at the half way stage, Kingham railway Station lies ahead of you here, through the village).

Otherwise continue, passing through Daylesford, to reach the A436 in 1.5 miles. Turn left to cross the railway, and then first left in a quarter of a mile, into Lower Oddington. Cycle through the village, and its neighbour of Upper Oddington, to reach the B4450. Turn left and right and in a quarter of a mile, having crossed the old railway bridge, follow the lane for 1 mile up to Icomb.

Continue through the village, climbing up to the A424. Go across at the offset crossroads, and then turn right at another crossroads in 1 mile with airfield houses to your left. Whiz down through Little Rissington, to reach Bourton-on-the-Water in 2 miles.

## Section 3: Bourton-on-the-Water to Cherington

Leave Bourton-on-the-Water, by turning off the main street at the head of the greens, over the stream, by the museum. This lane soon begins to climb; continue up onto the ridge, and cycle ahead for 3 miles to reach Farmington. Bear right at the village green and then first left after 400 yards. You reach Northleach, with a good descent, in 1.5 miles, having passed under the A40.

Leave Northleach by Millend, passing the mill remains, ignoring a small right turn after a few yards. Continue for 1.5 miles and go across at an offset junction. In 1 mile you reach Coln St.Dennis, before crossing the stream, and bearing left to cycle parallel with the stream. (The next few miles involve many crossings of this stream; as long as you continue to follow it you'll be cycling in the right direction!) In just over half a mile you reach Coln St.Rogers.

Turn left at a small 'T' junction, after a crossroads, to cross the stream, and then right after 300 yards to cross the stream again. You then pass through Winson, cycling parallel with the water again. Continue for 1 mile before turning first left to cross the stream again, into Ablington, bearing right to reach Bibury in 1 mile.

## The Coln Valley around Bibury

Many of the lanes in this area are perfect for cycling, though the villages can become clogged with cars in the tourist season. If you can reach Bibury at a quieter time of day it is a lovely spot. Try to incorporate a visit to the museum. In particular this has a selection of art and other items associated with William Morris. Arlington Row, the subject of so many postcards, is another attraction, if you can get a look in!

Having visited and explored Bibury, leave by the B4425 for Cirencester. In a quarter of a mile, at a five-way junction, turn left. At the first junction in 1 mile turn right, and then bear right almost immediately, to reach Barnsley in 1.5 miles. Bear left onto the 'B' road and then take the second right into the centre of the village, once the main road has swung left.

## Barnsley

There are two places you should make time for in this village. One is Barnsley House and gardens, for while the house itself is not open to the public, the gardens are, and provide a scented floral history lesson. Details of opening hours from 0285 740281.

The church is the second stopping place in the village. Built on a rise, you will see it from several miles away. There are wonderfully horrible Norman faces and figures both outside and inside the building.

To leave Barnsley, go across at a small crossroads after 200 yards, having turned right off the main street. Continue for 1 mile to bear right at a small junction and cycle on for 1 mile to reach the A429. Cross the 'A' road, with CARE, and continue for 1.5 miles, going ahead at a crossroads after 1 mile, to reach the A435. Go across here; slightly left, into the lane.

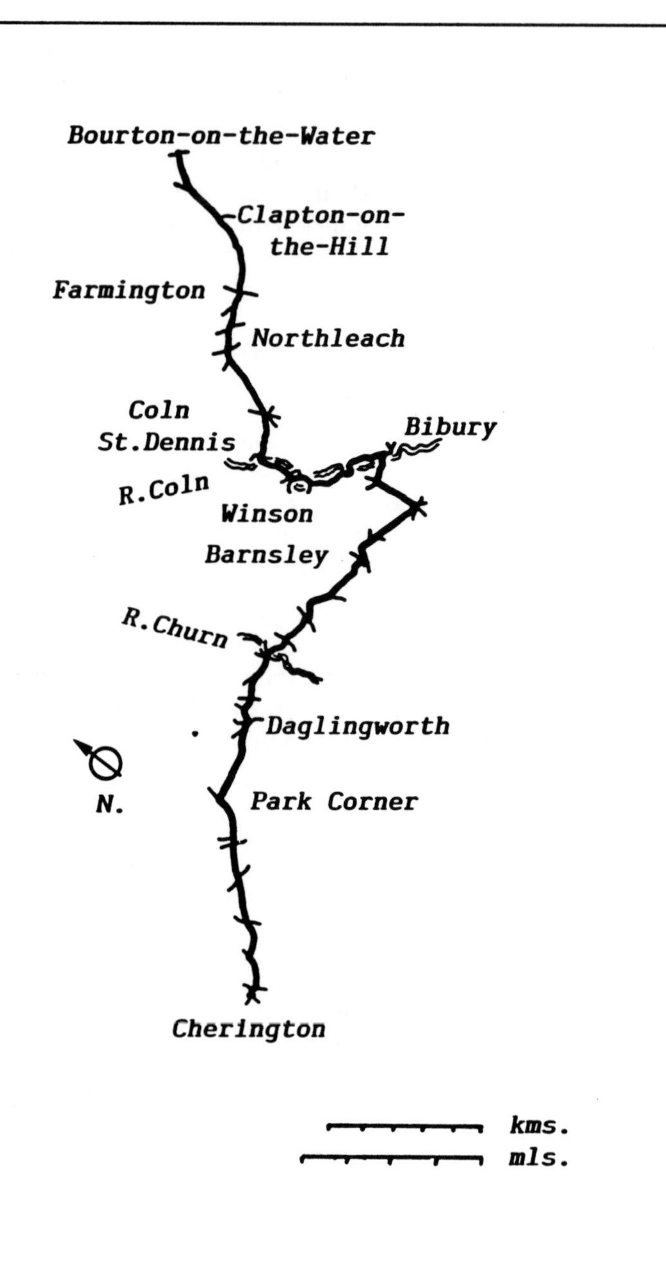
Bourton-on-the-Water
Clapton-on-
the-Hill
Farmington
Northleach
Coln
St.Dennis
Bibury
R.Coln
Winson
Barnsley
R.Churn
Daglingworth
N.
Park Corner
Cherington
kms.
mls.

Go ahead at the immediate crossroads, ignore a right after half a mile, to reach the A417 in 1 mile. Across, with CARE, here at the slightly offset junction, to arrive at Daglingworth in half a mile.

Turn right at the small 'T' junction, and then bear left out of the village, ignoring a small right after 100 yards. Continue for 2 miles, passing through woods and reaching a 'T' junction once you have cleared the trees. This is called Park Corner, because it's at the corner of Cirencester Park!

To continue from Park Corner, turn left and continue for 1 mile to a crossroads, at which you go ahead for half a mile to reach the A419. In 1 mile go ahead at an offset crossroads, and continue for 1.5 miles to reach Cherington.

## Section 4: Cherington to Bath

Turn right and then bear left through the village of Cherington, passing the church. In half a mile, having ignored the first small right, turn right and continue for 2 miles to reach the B4014. Go across here, and in half a mile at a 'T' junction, turn right. Continue for 2 miles to reach the A46, where you cycle across, with CARE, into a lane. Follow this lane as it bears right, and then left, to arrive in Kingscote in 1 mile. Turn first left in the village to reach the A4135. Turn left and first right – with CARE, by the pub. Turn first left after a quarter of a mile. Continue for 1 mile, cycling into, and then out of, the combe at Newington Bagpath. At a small 'T' junction, turn right to reach the A46 in half a mile. Cross the 'A' road, with CARE, and cycle on for 2 miles before turning first right. Continue for 1.5 miles to reach Leighterton.

## Leighterton

This small, pretty, but busy working village is an ideal site for a pause. There are several good barns and houses and a fine church. Just off the route, to the right of the village as you cycle through, you can spot the site, surrounded by a stone wall, of the highest long barrow in the Cotswolds. This may suggest that your route is downhill from now on; your are broadly right but there are a few more wrinkles before the descent into the Avon valley at Bath.

To continue from Leighterton, turn first left before the church and then ahead; second exit to leave the village. After two miles you reach a junction by the A433. Turn right here, but NOT along the 'A' road, to pass through Didmarton. At the A433 again go across, with CARE. Bear right after 1 mile and then first left in a quarter of a mile. Turn left at a 'T' junction in less than 1 mile to reach Little Badminton. Continue around the edge of the park to arrive at Badminton in 1 mile. Turn first right in the village, and continue for half a mile to cross the railway, by Acton Turville. Wind through the village and then take the B4039 to cross the motorway. Having crossed the motorway, turn first right, and then second left after 150 yards. After a further 400 yards go across an offset small crossroads, into Nettleton Green.

To continue from Nettleton Green, cycle ahead through the village before turning right after the 'phone box. Pass through the hamlet of West Kington, bearing left at the fork and then continuing for 1 mile to a crossroads. Turn right here and continue for over 1 mile to a 'T' junction. Turn left here and first right in half a mile. Turn right at the second small crossroads which you reach in 1 mile. After 1.25 miles you reach the A46 with Dyrham Park ahead and to your right. To continue turn left onto the 'A' road, and then first right, with CARE, after 150 yards. Continue for 1.25 miles to a widened and offset junction with the A420. Go across, with CARE, here and continue for 1.5 miles, going ahead at a crossroads. At a junction 200 yards after this crossroads bear left. Continue for 1 mile, ignore a right turn shortly after the racecourse, and in half a mile you will see Beckford's Tower very clearly on your right.

## Beckford's Tower

William Beckford was a collector, author, traveller and scholar who lived from 1760-1844. He was a rich man and used much of his wealth to

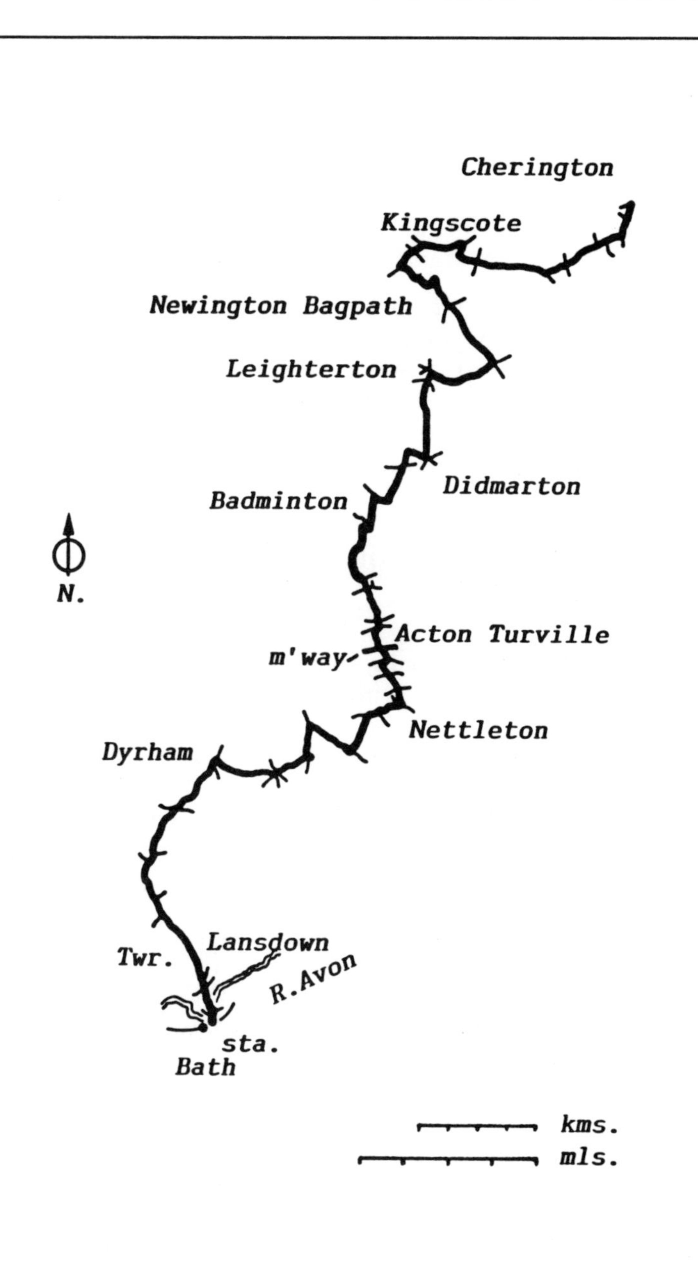
Cherington
Kingscote
Newington Bagpath
Leighterton
Didmarton
Badminton
N.
Acton Turville
m'way
Nettleton
Dyrham
Lansdown
Twr.
R.Avon
sta.
Bath
kms.
mls.

establish collections for public display and the buildings in which to house them. The 154 foot tower looked out over Beckford's other properties, while the base formed a 'study-retreat'.

The tower is open on weekend afternoons from April to October. If you arrive at other times the view from the base, and that of the tower itself, and still impressive. For further details, or to arrange a special visit, 'phone 0225 312917.

Continue downhill from the tower into Bath, along Lansdown Road. At the first junction in the city you are only half a mile from the station. To reach it, go ahead into Broad Street, bearing left to Northgate Street. Turn right here into the High Street. Ahead of you are the baths and the Tourist Office. Turn left here round the Orange Grove, to turn right into Pierpoint Street. Continue ahead into Manvers Street, and Bath Spa Station is ahead of you.

## Bath to Bristol by Cycle Path

For the cycle path link from Bath to Bristol proceed as follows:

Leave the city centre on the main road to the west. (There is also an alternative, signposted, backroads route to link up with the cyclepath, but this can be confusing). The name of this road changes several times but it is also signed as the A4 to Bristol. It becomes the Upper Bristol Road. After 1.5 miles turn left into Locksbrook Road. As this in turn becomes Brassmill Lane you will see the signs to take you onto the cyclepath. This continues very certainly and safely into Bristol. Having followed the signs for Bristol the cyclepath will bring you back to normal tarmac at Trinity Street/St.Phillip's Road, only a quarter of a mile from Bristol Temple Meads Station. The route on to the station is signed from here.

If you wish to park your cycle at the station while you explore Bristol, supervised storage, for which you have to pay, and un-supervised racks, which are free, are both available.

*Beckford's Tower, Bath*

# Appendix

## Tourist Information Centres

These centres will give expert information and advice on their area. The area they cover, and therefore know best, is sometimes rather quirky; boundaries can follow local authority or county lines, rather than the country's natural divisions. For example the Windrush valley is covered by Burford and Witney, but also Stow-on-the-Wold, as there is not an information centre in Bourton-on-the-Water to cover the western section! Some will be responsible for a large 'patch'.

The larger T.I.C.s also offer a B.A.B.A. scheme which stands for book a bed ahead. For a £1 fee they will book you in to a recommended bed and breakfast further along your route.

Another piece of advice concerns Tourist Board Approved accommodation. While this is all inspected and of excellent quality, the listings are only of members and a payment is required. It is a listing not a directory. There are many other places to stay in each area which may not be listed and yet still offer good quality and value for money. The Tourist Board will not thank me for saying this but it is the case!

Finally, as well as the official advice and information providers, the people that you meet on the road, locals in pubs, fellow users of accommodation, and perhaps above all other cyclists you meet on your way, will all be happy to help if approached in the right way. A smile, a 'please' and a 'thank you' will get you the best service.

A list of addresses of T.I.C.s in the area covered by this book is to be found on the next two pages.

| | |
|---|---|
| Bath | The Collonades, 11-13 Bath Street, Avon<br>BA1 1SW<br>Tel: 0225 462831 |
| Bristol | 14 Narrow Quay, Bristol, Avon BS1 4QA<br>Tel: 0272 260767 |
| Broadway | 1 Cotswold Court, Broadway,<br>Worcestershire WR12 7AA<br>Tel: 0386 852937 |
| Burford | The Brewery, Sheep Street, Burford,<br>Oxfordshire OX8 4LP<br>Tel: 0993 823558 |
| Cheltenham | 77 Promenade, Cheltenham,<br>Gloucestershire GL50 1PP<br>Tel: 0242 522878 |
| Chipping Campden | Woolstaplers Hall Museum, High Street,<br>Chipping Campden ,<br>Gloucestershire GL55 6HB |
| Cirencester | Corn Hall, Market Place, Cirencester,<br>Gloucestershire GL7 2NW<br>Tel: 0285 654180 |
| Faringdon | The Pump House, 5 Market Place, Faringdon,<br>Oxfordshire SN7 7HL<br>Tel: 0367 242191 |
| Gloucester | St Michael's Tower, The Cross, Gloucester,<br>Gloucestershire GL1 1PD<br>Tel: 0452 421188 |
| Malmesbury | Town Hall, Cross Hayes, Malmesbury,<br>Wiltshire SN16 9BZ<br>Tel: 0666 823748 |
| Northleach | Cotswold Countryside Collection,<br>Northleach, Gloucestershire GL54 3JH<br>Tel: 0451 60715 |

| | |
|---|---|
| Oxford | St Aldgates, Oxford,<br>Oxfordshire OX1 1DY<br>Tel: 0865 726871 |
| Painswick | The Library, Stroud Road, Painswick,<br>Gloucestershire GL6 6DT<br>Tel: 0452 813552 |
| Stow-on-the-Wold | Hollis House, The Square,<br>Stow-on-the-Wold,<br>Gloucestershire GL54 1AF<br>Tel: 0451 831082 |
| Stratford-upon-Avon | Bridgefoot, Stratford-upon-Avon,<br>Warwickshire CV37 6GW<br>Tel: 0798 293127 |
| Stroud | Subscription Rooms, George Street,<br>Stroud, Gloucestershire GL5 1AE<br>Tel: 0453 765768 |
| Swindon | 32 The Arcade, Brunel Centre,<br>Swindon, Wiltshire SN1 1LN<br>Tel: 0793 530328 |
| Winchcombe | Town Hall, High Street, Winchcombe,<br>Gloucestershire GL54 5LJ<br>Tel: 0242 602925 |
| Witney | Town Hall, Market Square, Witney,<br>Oxfordshire OX8 6AG<br>Tel: 0993 775802 |

Cycling Notes & Diary

Cycling Notes & Diary

## Cycling Notes & Diary